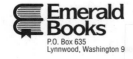

Emerald
Books
P.O. Box 635
Lynnwood, Washington 9

SURVIVING THE PRODIGAL YEARS
Copyright © 1995 Marcia Mitchell
All rights reserved

ISBN 1-883002-12-5

Published by Emerald Books
P.O. Box 635
Lynnwood, Washington 98046

Printed in the United States of America

For my Dad

William (Bill) Dummler

Thank you for being such a wonderful parent.

I love you, Dad!

CONTENTS

Chapter One

A SHATTERING MOMENT

IT CAN HAPPEN in the blink of a turn signal, in the slam of a door, in the ring of a telephone. In one brief moment, your life can disintegrate. One minute you are dealing with the day-to-day struggles of raising a family and generally keeping up with life, and suddenly your world is shattered. A tidal wave of emotion hurls you into the midst of a raging sea—your daughter, your son, is trapped by the octopus of rebellion, drugs, prostitution, or crime, or your child has run away.

Volumes have been written on how to raise a teenager, how to train up a child, how to be a loving parent. But when my teenage daughter ran away from home and sucked the family into the vortex of her rebellion, I was unable to find comfort or guidance. In one tragic moment, my life was shattered. In an instant, the dreams I'd held for my daughter vanished.

Parents all hope that one day their children will mature to a state of independence from them. They nurture their children, molding and shaping them so that the time will come when they can stand alone and become productive adults. No healthy-minded parent wants his or her children to remain dependent forever. But sometimes the break comes too soon. Children will wrench themselves out of their parents' control, perhaps even fling themselves from the nest, defy their parents' instruction and revolt against their training. The child of Independence says, "I have learned from you and am strong enough now to walk alone." But the child of Rebellion says, "I don't want your training, and although I may not be ready to walk alone, I'm willing to take my chances without you."

For every child who rebels, the life of at least one other person—and, most often, the lives of two or more other people (the parents and family)—is shattered. In the crush, the Christian parent will face God, clamoring for answers to spiritual questions. As one recovering parent to another, I'd like to share some of the help God has given me for the spiritual dilemmas that we all face during our children's prodigal years.

THE SHOCK OF LEARNING THE TRUTH

I have to be honest with you. I really thought I had it all together. I mean really! I knew where my children were and what they were doing at all times (at least I thought I did). I attended PTA and school programs and prodded my children until their homework was done. My children went to church with me every week. They attended church camp in the summer and faithfully memorized Scripture verses. I lived in a pink bubble, believing that because I was doing all the right things, nothing could happen to my children—at least not all that ugly stuff you read about in the newspapers.

"Drunk Teen Crashes Truck, 2 Killed!"
"Teen Crack House Raided"
"High School Prostitute Ring Revealed"

Those are other people's kids. My kids wouldn't do any of those things. They wouldn't even think about them.

Although my job at the county juvenile court opened my eyes to a world that I never knew existed, even that didn't prepare me. There were real kids who got into real trouble and created those headlines. But I never once thought a child of mine could be like that. The two worlds—my pink bubble at home and the reality of teens in trouble—were totally separated in my mind.

I should have been prepared…but I wasn't!

I should have seen the signs…but I didn't!

I didn't know my world was about to fall apart. I didn't know that rebellion seethed beneath a veneer of "normal" life, straining to break through.

The shock, when it came, was total and devastating! One typical day, without warning, my daughter disappeared—just walked away from school and vanished! With the force and suddenness of Mount St. Helen's eruption, my pink bubble of security burst, and I suddenly found myself on very shaky ground spiritually. Where was God when all this was going on? Where was He now that my world was shattered? I felt betrayed by the One who had Himself been betrayed.

I know I'm not the only one who has been catapulted into the chaos of a child's rebellion. I'm not the first to go through it, and I definitely won't be the last. But when it comes (notice I said when, not if), how does one survive? Mentally, emotionally, physically, spiritually—how does one survive? We won't come through it unscarred, but with Jesus' help, we can survive.

Living with a rebellious teenager is like watching the old-time film, *The Perils of Pauline*. Every week you can expect a real cliff hanger! My friend Donna learned that only too well. A Christian woman, Donna has a firm grasp on God and is a deeply trusted spiritual leader in our community. Her story, like mine, began with a single shattering moment. When her phone rang in the middle of the night, Donna had no hint that her world had already collapsed.

"I remember the red LED numbers on my bedside clock glared 2:02 a.m.," she told me. "If I hadn't been holding the telephone in my hand, I'd have thought it was a nightmare!"

As her car raced toward the hospital, Donna's only thought was for her daughter Heather. How badly was she hurt? What had happened? Was she alive? The police, with no explanation, had only said to meet them in the emergency room. When Donna arrived at the hospital, she learned that Heather had overdosed on drugs at a party in a tawdry apartment.

"Her life hung in the balance," Donna said, "and I didn't even know how it had happened. She was supposed to be spending the night with a friend. Since I knew both her friend and the family very well, I hadn't checked it out. It never occurred to me that Heather wasn't telling the truth."

In answer to prayer, Heather's life was spared that night but Donna would never be the same. Her bubble of security had burst, and nothing would ever restore it. Unfortunately, in the years to come, that was not the only night that Donna would head for the emergency room of that hospital. But time after time, as she followed a howling ambulance to the hospital, she would pray, "God, spare her life. Just let her live. Let me try one more time."

Peace in the Midst of the Storm

Like the rest of us with problem children, Donna would find her greatest source of strength in quiet moments of prayer and devotion. When we are crying out, "Why me? Why this? Where are you, God? Why did you let this happen?", the only way we can hear an answer is in the quiet moments alone with Him.

The nightmare of drugs has left deep scars on the lives of Donna's family. Whether it's drugs or something else, rebellion in any form ravages the lives of those connected to it. The scars run deep, the night is dark and we feel like we can't find our way. But in the depths of God's Word, we can find examples to follow when our own path is so dark we can't possibly find our way. There we can find promises to claim when our hope is gone, words of strength and comfort when we are utterly drained, and warnings that guide us onto the right path when we might stray.

When we find ourselves in the midst of a crisis, Scripture can sometimes provide the only beam of light. There was a time in the life of Christ when He chose to cross the lake, and He asked the disciples to go with Him.

"Let us go over to the other side," He said. Notice the phrase "Let us go…" He wanted the disciples to accompany Him. Since Jesus knew all things, He knew what lay just ahead. Yet He still chose to go and still invited the disciples along.

Unknowingly, the disciples jumped right into the boat and set off for the far shore, their fledgling faith yet untried. They left the crowds behind and took Him just as He was, and I assume they went just as they were. There wasn't any great flurry of preparation, no in-depth lecture from Jesus expounding on all the possibilities that might lie ahead. Blindly, the disciples pushed off from shore, accompanied by a few other boats.

That's how I entered parenthood—blindly, trusting that everything would be great. Because I couldn't have children of my own, two precious baby girls became part of our family through adoption. Those first years were just about the way I'd planned. "You see," I smirked to God. "If everyone would follow Christian principles in their parenting, everything would turn out just fine." That self-satisfaction was the lull before the storm.

The disciples were just as blind, just as lulled as I was. Just when they thought everything was going fine (after all, Jesus was asleep, wasn't he?), their world fell apart. A sudden squall swooped down on them in a furious onslaught. The wind tore at the sea, sending waves crashing over the sides of the boat in an attempt to sink it.

I can picture the disciples, drenched and bailing furiously. Shouting at each other above the torrents of rain and fierce wind to bail faster, they suddenly realize that something is missing. Where in all of this fury is their leader—the one who invited them into this storm? Incredibly, He lay fast asleep on a cushion in the stern. Looks of disbelief must have swept across the disciples' faces. Was it possible for anyone to sleep through such a storm? In panic, they sought His help. "Teacher," they woke Him, "don't you care if we drown?"

As only Christ could do, He rose and rebuked the storm. Into the face of its fury He uttered those golden words: "Quiet! Be still!" The wind and the waves responded to the Creator's voice, suddenly and completely slipping back into the confines that the Master had decreed (Mark 4:35-39).

I can't get over the fact that Jesus invited the disciples into that storm! He knew it was coming, yet He led them into it anyway. He knew the disciples didn't know what was ahead. It seems almost cruel, like a punishment, yet they hadn't done anything wrong. In fact, they'd been doing things right. So why did He insist they go through that storm? Couldn't He have avoided it? Apparently He chose for them to go through the storm, knowing their faith needed to grow.

What does all this have to do with drugs and the police calling in the middle of the night? You see, rebellion strikes in much the same way. Like a hurricane, it swoops down, lashing out at the family boat. Sometimes I feel like I'm right in the middle of that storm. Bailing frantically alongside the disciples, I find Jesus calmly sleeping in my boat! I don't even know where the storm is coming from. But there I am, sailing along on a smooth sea, savoring the latest spiritual message...when...WHAM! Suddenly, without warning, the storm breaks around me, in all its fury and I'm sinking fast. In panic I scream, "God, don't you care that I am drowning?" I only wish His response to me had been as swift and as simple as it was for the disciples.

When the phone rings in the middle of the night, it's a good indication you're already sinking—and you didn't even know a storm was brewing. When our kids are in trouble, storms are never gradual and mild, only sudden and devastating.

Each person's storm has its own peculiarities. None of us has exactly the same storm. Donna's storm was in the fight for her daughter's life in a hospital. Others, like Arturo, had to fight a daily onslaught. Arturo's son would come home at all hours of the night, flying high, only to crash the next day. No matter what Arturo did as a father, he couldn't reach his son with the truth of what he was doing to himself—literally blowing his mind! We experience agonies beyond compare when we must stand by in anguish, watching someone we dearly love deliberately destroy him or herself.

"Jesus, where are You?" was my heart's cry when I hung up the receiver from my own first devastating phone call. "Jesus, are you asleep? My world is crashing in on me, and I can't find you!"

Like the disciples I started bailing, using all the techniques I had, but it was all in my own strength. I called my friends in the police department for information and help. My former co-workers in the county juvenile department could only offer advice; there was nothing they could do to calm the storm.

Why is it that we often try so hard to deal with a crisis ourselves instead of going immediately to God? It took me a very long time to finally seek the real guidance God had for me. Only then did I experience inner peace.

REJOICE!

In the beginning of my daughter's prodigal years, before I had the courage to share my burden with others, I sometimes had to grit my teeth when I'd hear well-meaning Christians, as they'd pat someone on the back, say, "Well, Praise the Lord anyway!" or when the pastor would preach a sermon on Philippians 4:4: "Rejoice in the Lord always. I will say it again: Rejoice!"

How can you praise God when you're a breath away from collapsing under the strain? Where is the praise in wondering whether or not your child will be rational the next time you see him or her? Surely God doesn't expect a song of joy to burst from our lips when our child comes dragging in at 4:00 a.m. reeking of marijuana or glassy-eyed and stumbling up the stairs.

And yet, how do we handle this verse in the Bible? Do we just ignore it? I, for one, rather than accept its truth for me, assumed it applied to all those glowingly happy Christians I saw in church every week. But the Holy Spirit wouldn't let me do that. He forced me to face this Scripture squarely. He wasn't giving me a choice. He was giving me a command! Do it!

Rejoice!

Not just if and when you want to, but always!

Now a command is a bit difficult to ignore, especially when it's issued by the Holy Spirit. In fact, when God commands that we do something, do we dare disobey? Believe me, I didn't like the train of thought the Holy Spirit was following any more than most of you probably do right now. Does this mean that I was disobeying God because I wasn't praising Him?

Somehow the phrase, "Thank you, God, that my son or daughter is using drugs," just didn't ring true. And personally, even if I forced myself to say those words, I couldn't bring myself to mean them. So what do we do with a command that seems impossible to obey?

"God must mean something else," I muttered, flipping the pages of my Bible to check a cross-reference. "He can't possibly mean for us to praise Him in circumstances like these." My fingers stopped at James 1:2-3: "Consider it pure joy, my brothers, whenever you face trials of many kinds, because you know that the testing of your faith develops perseverance."

As soon as I read that verse I wanted to relegate it into the "ignore" category. But then a little word leapt out at me. "When," not "if," but *when* you face trials. In other words, God knows we are going to have trials. We are to expect them, and now He's telling us how to behave when they happen.

I quickly recalled the story of Jesus and the disciples in that boat on the stormy lake. Jesus knew that a storm would come, and the disciples should have known it was a possibility. Jesus doesn't call us to a life of ease. But knowing trials will come, He shows us how to behave when the storms do hit.

Suddenly I had a mental picture of the disciples bailing furiously, but instead of panicking or shouting at each other above the wind, they're rhythmically scooping water to a rousing rendition of the Hallelujah Chorus! (I know God has a sense of humor when He allows such an image to flash through my mind.)

A bit more seriously, I tried harder to make an application of these two verses in my life. Obviously, if God knows we will have trials and we should plan on their coming, His command to "rejoice always" includes our storms. I don't think the disciples rejoiced because of the storm; I believe they experienced peace when they allowed Jesus to take control of the storm. And peace is something for which we can always praise God.

The more I thought about it, the more I realized that like the disciples, I had Jesus right there with me in the midst of my storm. He was just waiting for me to call on Him. He wanted to bring peace and calm into my storm.

Slowly, obediently, I formed the words these verses commanded. "Thank you, Jesus, for being with me in my storm." As His calmness settled over me, the Holy Spirit added more praises, like building blocks: "Thank you that the situation isn't any worse than it is. Thank you that she isn't dead. Thank you for the Scripture that offers me hope." And then, strangely, I heard my own voice add, "Thank you for this situation that has allowed me to take a new step in my relationship with You."

Could that really be me? I couldn't thank Him for the pain and agony of the storm, but I could say, "I'm rejoicing in my newfound relationship in Jesus." There was the very answer I sought. The Holy Spirit had gently guided me into learning a way to rejoice always.

FACING REALITY AND CLAIMING GOD'S PROMISES

Even as I had to change my view of the life I thought my daughter was living, so Donna, in the months following Heather's overdose, had some realities to face. The precious child she had cuddled and nurtured had been replaced by a teenage stranger. Donna learned that her daughter had been living a completely separate life when she was away from home. Heather, like many of our children, had succumbed to the pressures of her peer group, crossing into a realm of existence that most people are only vaguely acquainted with through the news stories.

Over the months, Donna sought and found an inner strength that allowed her to find God's praise even in this storm. Only Donna and the Holy Spirit knew all the steps it had taken to get her to that point. Donna, like the rest of us, realized that even as Jesus brought peace to the wind and the waves, so He can bring peace to all of His creation. Although we can't always see the reason for what happens, we can attempt to yield our situation to His control. If we will let Him, He will control our storms, never allowing them to gain in intensity beyond what we are able to bear. No storm is too fierce for Him to control or too furious to resist His calming voice.

All we need to do is call on Him, claiming the promises so lavishly displayed throughout the Bible. If God's Word is true—and I believe it is—then logically every promise in the Bible is available to us. Our obedience comes in seeking the promises (reading the Bible and praying). Then, we are to claim those promises—live them out in our lives. As Jesus invited the disciples to go into the storm with Him, dare to recognize that He has invited you into whatever your current storm is. Release His power by calling on Him.

King David lived a life filled with storms. In agony he called on God for deliverance and peace. Out of his painful experiences he penned a blessing that bears repeating in the first verse of Psalm 20. "May the LORD answer you when you are in distress."

Each of us will find many promises in the Bible that will be tailored to our own needs with very personal meanings. At the end of every chapter, I will be sharing questions for thought, a prayer to pray, and a promise for you to claim. May I suggest that you take the time to search out the personal implications of the promise through the power of the Holy Spirit and let that promise become a stepping-stone to a closer relationship between you and God.

■ ■ ■

1. What kind of storm are you currently experiencing?

2. How are you reacting?

3. What do you plan to do to allow Jesus to bring you peace and calm in the midst of your storm?

PRAYER TO PRAY

Heavenly Father, You who love Your own children even in their rebellion, cradle now my own rebellious child. As this storm rages through my life, come and be my calm. Help me to remember that You have not abandoned me but are even now standing beside me. Help me to remember, too, that You have not abandoned my child either. May Your peace permeate my home, my family, and most of all my heart. Amen.

PROMISE TO CLAIM

"And surely I am with you always...."
(Matthew 28:20)

Chapter Two

THE WRONG CHILD

"YOU MUST BE MISTAKEN," JoAnn shook her head at the officer standing on her porch. "My son wouldn't do anything like this. Our last name is very common, so you must have us mixed up with someone else."

"But you do have a son named John?" the officer patiently asked again. When she nodded he added, "His birthdate and description match these?" He held up the form.

"Yes," JoAnn nodded again. "Who gave you his birthdate?"

"He did, ma'am"—the officer kept his voice soft and even, waiting for the reality to sink in—"at the time he was apprehended."

"But...burglary? That just isn't possible!"

"Sorry, ma'am." The officer chose not to argue but stated, "Your son's at the station now. Could you follow me down there and pick him up?"

"He's...Johnny's at the police station? Right now?" JoAnn stood stock still. "Why is he there? I just told you he wouldn't do such a thing. My Johnny's a good boy."

JoAnn quickly found her purse and hurried after the officer. "They have the wrong boy," she muttered to the rearview mirror in her car. "My son wouldn't steal anything. I've raised him better than that. Besides, he goes to church all the time."

Again, she shook her head. "I don't know who they are holding in that police station, but for sure it isn't my Johnny."

In their small town, it took only a few minutes to reach the police station. Once inside, JoAnn followed the officer down a short flight of stairs and into a sterile cubicle. Her son sat in a large oak chair across the desk from another police officer.

"Son?" JoAnn stopped short. "It is you. I was sure they had you mixed up with someone else."

"Please have a seat," The second officer indicated another chair. "I'd like to go over these forms with both you and your son, just to be sure you understand what is happening."

"I'm sure you've made a mistake, officer." She hesitated, resting a hand on the back of the chair.

"Please sit down," he motioned. "We have quite a bit to discuss."

An hour later, JoAnn left the police station with her son. Alone with him in the car, she finally spoke. "Johnny, tell me what really happened. I don't know how you got mixed up in this, but I know you wouldn't take anything that wasn't yours."

They moved slowly through traffic, but JoAnn kept her attention on her son. When he didn't answer right away, she prompted, "Son?"

"Uh, you're right, Mom." He squirmed a bit on the seat. His words blurted out all in one breath, tumbling on top of each other. "I didn't do it. I was just standing there talking to Keith when the cop came up. See, Keith had this pillowcase in his bike basket. I don't know where he got the stuff, but 'cause I was there, the cop took me, too."

"Of course, dear." JoAnn sighed in relief. "Besides, weren't you at the ballgame when all this was supposed to have happened?"

"Uh…yeah. I was." John looked away from her, seeming to be interested in something that was happening outside the car.

"Well, don't you worry." JoAnn turned the car into their driveway, "We'll get this cleared up right away. But in the meantime, young man, I don't want you to have anything to do with this boy Keith."

"Sure, Mom. Uh, can we go out for hamburgers tonight?"

FROM DENIAL…

Blind denial is often our first reaction to being confronted with the reality of our children's rebellion. We all want to believe that our children are innocent, especially when the encounter with the law is our first. We just can't believe our children would do anything wrong. Of course, when the children turn those innocent-puppy eyes on us, we'll believe anything they say. They are quick, too, to follow our lead. If we deny the truth, they will tell us what we want to hear.

It's later, much farther down the road when we learn the truth, that our trust in those beautiful eyes wavers and becomes cynical disbelief. Finally, we sink to never believing anything they say until positive proof is given, and even then our belief is reluctant. But somewhere between trust and distrust, belief and disbelief, most of us must wade through the steps of denial and manipulation.

...TO MANIPULATING THE LAW...

The first thing I tried to do when we were slammed up against the law was to manipulate the situation. I called my friends in the law enforcement field, attempting to keep everything as low-key as possible. I would excuse the incident by saying it was a one-time-only occurence.

I believed what my daughter said. Very quickly she learned that all she had to do was keep a straight face and blink those big eyes and I'd swallow everything she said. Later, when I saw my mistakes, I was ashamed of my gullibility.

Part of my problem came because I was a naive Christian. After all, I reasoned, I was a praying mother and thought that God wouldn't let my child do anything wrong, not when I'd spent all those hours praying for her...would He?

...TO MANIPULATING GOD...

The next step is trying to manipulate God. Why, oh why do we think God is some weak being who will yield to our every whim? When things are looking a bit stormy, we begin the manipulation. "Please God, just make this go away. I promise that I'll make sure my child doesn't get into any more trouble. I'll give more money to the church. I'll spend extra time praying for the missionaries..." and the list grows all out of proportion.

Why do we think that all we have to do is mumble the right words and God will jump through the hoop we hold in front of Him? We should know that as soon as we do something really foolish we can count on being confronted with the truth. Why we think we can get away with trying to manipulate God, I'll never know...except that all of us try it sometime in our life.

Manipulation never works. God will not become a puppet on anyone's string, whether a king or a desperate parent. Even though we may think for a few moments that God is doing what we want Him to do, there will come a point of reckoning. Count on it.

SEEK GOD'S WILL

Rather than try to manipulate God, we are to follow His command to seek His will for our lives. In the very basic prayer that Jesus used as a guideline for His disciples, He included the phrase, "your will be done on earth as it is in heaven" (Matthew 6:10). Above all else, the will of the Father is to take precedence.

Jesus again states, "But seek first his kingdom and his righteousness, and all these things will be given to you as well" (Matthew 6:33). This verse talks about our tendency to worry over details, but it also includes the same general principle that we are to seek God's will above our own.

Jesus applied this principle Himself in the garden of Gethsemane when He prayed, "My Father, if it is possible, may this cup be taken from me. Yet not as I will, but as you will" (Matthew 26:39). Even the Son of God did not attempt to manipulate the Father. Instead, He was honest in His feelings and desires but yielded willingly to the Father's plan.

Now, of course, this doesn't mean that we can't ask God to help us or to work in our lives. Jesus spent His life trying to teach us how much God cares about us and wants to work in us. Scripture is full of God's promises to hear and answer our prayers. But there is a condition that needs to be met first. The writer of the First Epistle of John affirms God's willingness to move on our behalf. "This is the confidence we have in approaching God: that if we ask anything according to his will, he hears us. And if we know that he hears us—whatever we ask—we know that we have what we asked of him" (I John 5:14-15).

Did you notice the condition? Right there on the page, in black and white, it says if we ask according to his will. Those words ought to be written in capital letters or at least underlined! We can ask, but it has to be for something that God would want to do in our situation. Sometimes that's a pretty tough order.

Often when we're in a state of panic or a very desperate situation, all we can think to say is, "God, get me out of this—NOW!" As we walk through the vaulted maze of a juvenile detention facility for the first time, it's not easy to stop and ask, "Okay, God, what is your will for me?" But we really have no other choice. God didn't say to ask according to His will if we feel like it. He said that was the only way we can be assured that He will hear us. So, how can we change our prayers?

GIVE IT TO GOD

It's better to place our problems in God's hands than it is to try to work them out ourselves. When left to ourselves, we generally only make matters worse. You are probably reading this book because you're currently in a very trying situation with a rebellious child. If you've attempted to work things out, to manipulate God, people, or the law, you know how quickly things can get really fouled up. Only God can make them work out for the very best.

To begin with, you honestly don't have all the facts. Oh, you may think you do. But the truth is, you'll probably never have all the facts. Every decision your child made along the path to where all of you are right now was influenced by a dozen different sources. Since you have no way of knowing all of them, your judgement is based on partial information.

On the other hand, God knows the full truth. He knows every influence on your child's life. He knows exactly what will bring about the necessary changes. Wouldn't it be better to leave all the details to the One who knows the full truth?

Another point to consider is that we view our problems in light of today's perspective while God views them in terms of eternity. I wish with all my heart that our children would live "normal" lives, fitting into society, attending church, and becoming stable, productive people. But God is more interested in their eternal living situation than He is in having them fit into current society. He knows exactly what it will take to confront them in the best way possible to give them every chance to become one of His—and that is what is most important. I'd rather have my children spend eternity in Heaven than live today in the finest castle, attend the grandest cathedral, or be president of a country or corporation.

FACE THE TRUTH

JoAnn had become ensnared in a trap that so many of us fall into—denying that our child could do any wrong. We wear blinders so firmly on the end of our noses that our sight is impaired.

It wasn't until she was in court that JoAnn was able to switch off the tunnel vision. She'd been so focused on what was happening now that she couldn't even consider for a moment that her son John might possibly be guilty of committing a crime. As the evidence was produced, she learned that John had been seen, along with his friend Keith, riding his bike across the victim's lawn and parking behind the house. Then, along with Keith, he had entered a basement window and together they had stolen quite a large amount of goods.

When confronted with the proof of John's fingerprints, which were found inside the victim's house, JoAnn had no choice but to recognize that her denial of her son's guilt didn't change the truth. John was guilty whether she wanted to believe it or not. Thus began an entirely different lifestyle for JoAnn (and for her son), but how unfortunate that she had to wait so long. Look at all the time she wasted, time that could have been better spent in seeking God's will for her life.

This doesn't mean we should always disbelieve our children. On the contrary, they need our support. But we need to be willing to keep our eyes open and seek the truth in each situation. Vocally affirm your love for your children but point out that you will openly listen to all sides in the situation.

YIELD TO GOD'S WILL

Let your children know how you are praying. Let them hear you, if possible, yielding to God's will rather than trying to manipulate God. I know that in many circumstances, the last thing your children want to hear is that you love them or that you are praying for them. But, in love, do it anyway!

Be open with the law enforcement official assigned to your case. Ask as many questions as you can. Although it's part of the official's job to keep you informed, many parents just don't ask. Let the official know you are willing to work with him or her. Quite often a number of alternatives are available, but until you get involved, the court can view your situation only through the information it receives from your child.

Most importantly, seek the guidance and wisdom that only God can give. God has the answers to all our questions; He knows what we need even before we ask (Matthew 6:8).

It is when we are on our knees that God can show us what we ought to ask. Through the power of the Holy Spirit, we can be guided beyond our self-centered, earthly focus and be moved into the flow of heavenly thoughts. As Jesus poured out His earthly needs, He was listening to the heavenly flow, yielding willingly to the Father.

In this kind of yielded attitude, God can release His power to work out the very best possible solution to whatever the current problem is. He has promised to hear and answer us. We need only to ask according to His will.

■ ■ ■

1. In what way have you been denying your child's responsibility in the current situation?

2. In what way have you been trying to manipulate God? The authorities? Other people?

3. How can you change the way you have been praying?

Prayer To Pray

Heavenly Father, there is no way I can possibly have all the facts in my current situation, but I know that You have them all and You understand the whole situation. I feel vulnerable. I want to believe that my child is not guilty. I just want to take my child home and forget this whole thing, but I know that's not possible. Help me to place all of this into Your hands. Help me to trust You for guidance. Most of all, I ask that You provide the very best answer for my child, the answer that will produce the greatest eternal value. Thank You for Your promise to hear and answer my prayers. Amen.

Promise To Claim

"Ask and it will be given to you; seek and you will find;
knock and the door will be opened to you. For
everyone who asks receives; he who seeks
finds; and to him who knocks,
the door will be opened."
(Matthew 7:7-8)

Chapter Three

LISTEN TO THE KIDS

The first time I smoked pot was about fourth grade," Brianna said. "A friend lived just a few blocks away and had an uncle who was into drugs. He just gave it to us. That's when it all started. I got kicked out of school for the first time when I was in the sixth grade."

Brianna's story ought to be shocking, but it isn't. Kids are getting involved in antisocial behavior at younger and younger ages. In times past, we could easily recognize which kids were at risk. Those who came from obviously dysfunctional families, whose parents were alcoholics, addicts, or absent, who came to school dirty and unkempt, if they came at all, were clearly likely to get involved in antisocial behavior themselves. In fact, it was a shock if they didn't.

WHO'S AT RISK?

Today, it isn't that easy to identify those who are at risk. Let's listen in as Rick, a director of a teen drop-in center, and his staff talk about kids in trouble.

Q. *What is your background, Rick?*

Rick: I come from an environment that was at best high risk for delinquency and alcohol and other drug abuse. I was raised in the inner city and became a gang member at an early age before I became a Christian.

Q. *Who is at risk and why?*

Rick: Everyone needs to feel accepted, cared for, and loved. Kids are at risk who experience lack of care, love and bonding. Gangs often fill those needs. A family history of alcoholism is another risk factor. Genetically, the predisposition to alcohol and other drug abuse is four times greater for the child of an alcoholic. Aside from this genetic predisposition to alcohol and other drug abuse are environmental factors. A study of adopted twins shows that the children carried these same rates of disposition to alcoholism.

Parental attitudes towards alcohol, and other drugs, and delinquency are important. The adolescent children of parents who favor the use of alcohol or other drugs or use recreational or heavy drugs are at a higher risk. Parents who are accepting of delinquent behavior fall into this same category. This would include people who say, "It's okay as long as you don't get caught," as well as the parent who is active in criminal and/or antisocial behavior.

Staff Member: Parents often forget what it was like to be nine years old—to have your whole world depend on what your friends think of you. Sometimes parents hand down commands without any rationale. Kids aren't dumb. Giving them a reason for a rule helps them to choose healthy behaviors.

We spend a lot of time talking about healthy relationships. We try to teach kids that it's not healthy when your friendship depends on what you wear, say, listen to, or watch. Parents often don't take time to explain their rationale. They forget that to a nine-year-old not having the right shoes might be as traumatic as an adult not having the right job.

Rick: Another risk factor is the alienation of the family. We hear a lot of "My parents just don't understand me." Or "I come here (to the Center) because you guys understand me." It's not that we have any more knowledge than the parents. We're probably more tuned in.

There are three more risk factors that are consistent with alcohol use as well as delinquency: low monitoring (some kids have no one at home with them), lack of guidelines (parents just don't tell their kids what is good or what's bad), and the flip side of that—excessive and severe discipline. These are very clear indicators of possible alcohol and delinquent problems.

Staff Member: Kids really rebel against parents' arbitrarily handing down commands. Rather than explaining to kids why they can't do a certain thing, the parents hand down rules in general. Kids understand reasons. Although they may not respect the rule, they'll respect you enough to follow the rule.

Inconsistency creates stress in a kid's life because the kid never knows from day to day what kind of punishment or consequences are going to result from his or her behavior.

THE ROLE OF THE FAMILY

Q. *How is the management of the family or environment important?*

Rick: Problems don't follow lines of economics or race. The affluent have problems, too. Some people think that these problems happen only in the lower socioeconomic areas, but that isn't true. Also, there is no indication that being a single parent in and of itself is a risk factor. When the single parent does not have time to set guidelines, monitor them, and give appropriate discipline, that's when problems arise. I have friends who were raised by single parents. Some went the wrong way, and others did well because their mothers took the necessary time for them.

Some risk factors just can't be eliminated, but you can reduce and buffer their effects. There is nothing you can do about who your biological parents are. Also, those kids who have problems in school become socially ostracized. They see those who are doing well in school as their enemies. Those kids who don't go to school are usually the ones who are already involved in antisocial behavior and are often older. Imagine a kid in the third, fourth, or fifth grade who doesn't go to school. The only ones the kid can hang around with are the 17- and 18-year-olds who are skipping school or no longer attending school.

PEER PRESSURE
AND PARENTAL INFLUENCE

Q. *What about peer pressure? Is that a strong factor?*

Rick: When one person is saying, "You can't be my friend and I won't have anything to do with you, if you don't____," that's pressure! Even the media exert pressure.

Staff Member: When the media are saying, "You have to look like Janet Jackson," and parents or counselors are saying, "Not everyone is going to look that way," that's big-time pressure! Kids go through incredible stress about their looks. "Does my hair look all right? Do my clothes look right?" A girl was crying one day because her family didn't have money to buy the right kind of tennis shoes. That's stress! When you have a kid in tears who can't participate in a group because she's so worried that she can't buy the right tennis shoes, that's intense peer pressure.

Rick: It's different for gang members. Kids are joining not so much because of pressure as they are for survival. They have no choice. There's no protection outside the gang. And at least they have a sense of belonging. I sat down with ten gang members individually and asked them, "What was the best time in your life?" Every one of them said, "The day I got my colors, the day I was accepted into this brotherhood."

Q. *What about the influence of parents?*

Rick: Developmentally, from birth to nine years old, children are very influenced by what their parents say and do. As they get beyond nine, up to sixteen, they become less influenced by their parents and are more influenced by others. Parental influence is still there, but it's more important now what their peers think. They start to let go of this type of peer pressure once they get their own identity at 17, 18, or 19.

HOPEFUL OR HOPELESS?

Q. *Is there a sense of hopelessness with today's kids?*

Rick: Look at the statistics in the inner cities. One of every four black males is going to die, be murdered, before he is eighteen. The kids know that, too; they're not stupid. They ask, "What does it matter? Why try to stay in school and follow these rules and try to get an education when I'm going to be dead by the time I'm eighteen? I might as well live in the fast lane and take somebody with me. Chances are I'm not going to make it so why even think about a future?"

The future is not in their minds. They are saying, "I don't care. It doesn't matter. I'm not going to make it." One of the campaigns in the inner cities is "Stay in school. Education's great, and the real market to education is your future." The kids are saying, "It doesn't matter—I have no future. I may not make it, so why can't I have money and Jaguars now 'cause I'm not going to make it."

WHERE IS GOD IN ALL THIS?

Q. *Does God play any part at all in these kids' lives?*

Rick: There is a respect of a God who loves people. Even gang members say, "You know that everybody is supposed to be real good on church day." They talk about, "My mom goes to church." That's the last time they want to mention that. They don't want to talk about Mom, and they don't want to get too deep into God.

Mothers and God are convicting to them. A lot of members don't even want their moms to know what is happening. That's one of the reasons they run away and stay away—because it becomes obvious. Their mom would know what they are doing. You'd be surprised how many people sell drugs but don't take them. You ask them why they do it, and you wonder how many mothers get financed through drug money. A lot of mothers depend on drug money because that's the only way they can make it with the younger kids.

THE PRODIGAL KIDS SPEAK

"Everyone should be quick to listen, slow to speak and slow to become angry, for man's anger does not bring about the righteous life that God desires" (James 1:19-20).

Listening is an important aspect of our Christian lives. Along with listening to what is happening in a teen drop-in center, let's listen to some of the kids who have been in trouble. Not all of these kids have made the turn-around in their lives yet, but most of them have progressed far enough that they have a better perspective about their behavior.

Brianna, Pablo, Jamal, and Sherry speak frankly about their lives.

Q. Tell me about your growing up years.

Pablo: My home was pretty normal, just Mom, Dad, and my sister. Really nothing outstanding.

Brianna: Both my parents were at home. I had four other sisters but didn't know my oldest sister until I was eight. Dad never told any of us about her, and she just showed up at our house when she turned eighteen.

Jamal: I was adopted when I was a baby. My adoptive parents were working middle-class people. Later they adopted a little girl, too.

Sherry: My home was very normal, with a working mom and dad and my older sister.

Q. *Did you ever attend church?*

Brianna: My mom and dad never went to church with us; they just got us up and put us on the church van.

Pablo: Yes, all the time.

Jamal: Mom took me and my sister with her every week to Sunday school and church. Dad didn't go more than once or twice a year.

Sherry: Yes, every time the church door was open! My mom and sister went, but not my dad. We were extremely active in church things. I began teaching first- and second-grade Sunday school class when I was in the eighth grade.

Q. *When did your rebellion start, and why?*

Brianna: I was seven or eight. That's when my oldest sister showed up unexpectedly. I always needed attention. I felt ignored. If my sisters had something that I wanted, my parents would tell them to give it to me so I would shut up. I tattled on my sisters but only to get attention.

Pablo: For me it was hard rock music. I was a teenager, but I wasn't a Christian then. I remember getting into the rock scene, being drawn into it because of the sound. I remember time and time again my mom coming into my room, and I'd have the music going and my mom would ask me why I listened to that stuff. She couldn't understand. I'd say, "Because I like the sound, or the beat." My mom would ask me if I listened to the words. I listened because I liked the sound, plus there was a great amount of peer pressure.

When I was in grade school I was really into country music because my parents were into country music. At a younger age you're more influenced by your parents. When I started junior high school, the kids found out that I listened to country music. The pressure to change was incredible. I came home one day and said, "That's it. I'm listening to rock music from now on because I want to be like them." I wanted to be accepted by my peers.

Jamal: It was in junior high school. I thought Dad was too strict. Mostly I wanted independence and freedom.

Sherry: It started because my dad didn't like my boyfriend when I was a senior in high school.

Q. *What type of antisocial behavior were you involved in?*

Brianna: At first it was smoking cigarettes when I was in grade school, but it quickly progressed to other drugs. I got in trouble with the law for stealing a car and burglarizing a house. That's when I started hanging out with the wrong crowd. I quit school in the eighth grade, and I haven't been in school since.

Pablo: Mostly defying my parents because of the music and wearing the clothes that went with it... black...and other stuff. I started wearing clothes that my friends were wearing, and my parents didn't understand. I should have said, "This is what's happening at school—this is what my friends do."

Jamal: I started skipping school with some other kids. They sometimes had a bottle of whiskey, and later it was pot. When my parents wanted to move me to another school, I ran away from home because I didn't want to leave my friends. For a while I was in foster care. That really opened my eyes. Other kids had really bad homes and living situations. It showed me what a nice home and family I had, but it didn't stop me from drinking or using pot.

Sherry: I smoked cigarettes and pot a little, but I was never a drinker. Mostly I skipped school and lied to my parents a lot. If I had told them the truth, they would never have let me go out with my boyfriend.

Q. *What were some of the rules at home to which you objected?*

Brianna: Because I was acting so badly, my parents sent me to live with my aunt and uncle. They allowed me to dress up and go out, and I didn't have to be in until one o'clock. I was fourteen at that time and would go out with my cousins, who were a couple years older than me. When I moved back home, I couldn't go out anymore. That's when I started taking off and staying out all night and partying. I would go home when I needed to shower and change clothes. My parents let that go on for a while; my dad would try to spank me, and they would yell and scream at me. That's when I quit school. Then they put me in foster care for nine months. After I got out of foster care, I went home and continued to do the same thing. I would stay gone for weeks at a time.

Jamal: I couldn't bring my friends home, at least not the kind of kids I hung around with. I couldn't stay out after 10 p.m., and I always had to tell my folks where I was going.

Sherry: The biggest thing was curfew. I had to be home at 11 p.m. on the weekends, and things were just getting started at that hour.

Q. *What was your relationship with your parents at that time?*

Pablo: My parents and I had this communication problem. All my parents saw was that their child was turning bad. I wanted to fit in with my friends, but I didn't explain that to my parents, so they didn't know that was why I was changing. They weren't telling me that they didn't want me to listen to this stuff because of the message or because of the connotations of wearing those clothes. We just didn't communicate.

Brianna: I hated them. I hated my dad so much because he was such a jerk. He would hit me; that was his way of trying to tell me to cool my crap. He would get in my face and smile when I was mad, and he knew that it really bugged me. I have a bad temper just like him, and one time I grabbed a knife and started chasing him around the house. I swore I was gonna kill him. My mom ran next door and called the police, and they came and took me away.

My mom always tried to help me. After I started running away, they would lock the doors and put bars on the windows so I couldn't get in to get my clothes. I would call my mom at work and tell her off. I broke several windows trying to get into the house. Down deep inside I felt sorry for my mom but I didn't care. I really didn't hate my mom, but I would tell her I did just to hurt her. I always tried to take advantage of her, but I didn't hate her.

Jamal: I knew I was hurting my mom, but I just blocked out any feelings. Dad was so strict and distant that we weren't close at all.

Sherry: I really loved them, but I was so busy between work and school that I didn't see them a lot. They were gone a lot, too. I never had a problem with my mom, but my dad was really hard on me. All he wanted me to do was go to school and work. He never wanted me to have fun.

Q. *How did you get your money for alcohol or other drugs?*

Brianna: I told my Mom I needed food or something else. Sometimes I just asked for the money, then sometimes I would bug her so much she would get so mad she would just give me money to shut me up.

Jamal: At first it was easy. My friend's mother had all the booze we wanted and didn't care if we drank it. Later I just ended up using people however I could. Stealing, too.

Sherry: It was never a problem, because I worked. The tough part was having to buy it for my boyfriend. He often was mean to me if I refused.

Q. *Did you think about God at all during your time of rebellion?*

Brianna: What I learned about God came from church, but my mom and dad didn't go to church, so when you just go once a week, it really doesn't do much for you. There was never any talk about God at home, either. My mom prays a lot now and reads the Bible. She started going to church after I was so far gone I couldn't be helped. When I started to straighten out, I went with her and was eventually baptized.

Jamal: Not really. I was so into getting what I wanted that God wasn't important to me.

Sherry: Because of my job I had to quit going to church, so God just wasn't important. I just didn't think about Him.

Q. *Are you still involved in antisocial behavior? If not, why did you stop?*

Pablo: No, in fact I'm helping other kids in trouble now. My changes came because of finally growing up, I think.

Brianna: I don't do anything now! I don't even smoke cigarettes anymore. I overdosed on crank, and that stopped everything. The drug took over that night. I was scared; they told me I was having a mild stroke when I went to the hospital. After that I started getting really nervous. I don't do drugs anymore because I need to be in total control of my body. If I don't have total control, I feel weird, and I can't handle it. That night really opened my eyes big time! After I got caught with the auto theft and the burglary, I went to detention and then to a girls' home. That opened my eyes to going to these places, and I stayed out of that kind of trouble after that.

Jamal: I still smoke pot sometimes and go drinking once a month or so. I feel like I'm not hurting anybody.

Sherry: I stopped when I broke up with my boyfriend. My new boyfriend didn't want any part of that.

Q. *Are there any residual problems from your prodigal years?*

Brianna: My short-term memory is gone because I smoked a lot of pot for years.

Pablo: I still like hard rock music. Petra is a hard rock group, and when I play it, the kids I work with love it. It's the sound they want to hear. They can't get over how hard it is, and yet it's Christian music. There's stuff out there that's even harder than Petra, and the kids ask me, "You play that? That's Christian music? No way!" I play it a few times so they can listen to the words, and it's incredible.

Jamal: I haven't been able to hold a job for very long at a time and have almost given up trying to find one. I didn't finish high school, so that's a problem in finding work. I'm not trained to do anything.

Sherry: I don't think so. I guess I really learned my lessons the first time around.

Q. *What is your relationship with your parents now?*

Pablo: Gratefully, it's fully restored, although I still dress differently than they do. I like the hard rock look but make sure the message on my shirt is Christian.

Brianna: I apologize to my mom all the time. I always am afraid I am going to hurt her feelings, and I am trying to make up for what I did in the past. I feel really bad for my mom. I'm a lot closer to Dad now, too, but it's not perfect.

Jamal: I know I hurt my mom, but we never really severed our ties. I see my mom several times a week, but I just don't have any common ground with my dad. The only thing I worry about is that my son who is now three years old won't have a strong relationship with his grandfather. I just can't seem to find a way to rebuild that relationship.

Sherry: It's really good. My mom's about my best friend now. I used to be petrified of my dad, but now I can joke around with him. That's probably because he sees the changes in me. I think he's mellowed a bit, too.

Q. *What do you think about God in your life now?*

Pablo: Becoming a Christian is the most important thing I ever did. Now I'm working hard to help kids see Christ in my life.

Brianna: I thank Him as much as I thank my mother. I don't talk to Him a lot. I pray sometimes, and I thank Him when I do.

Jamal: I think God is important enough to send my son to Sunday School and church every week with my mom.

Sherry: I'm back in church now. I got married four years ago, and this year I started having problems with my pregnancy and it scared me. That's when I really turned back to God. It seemed like God answered my prayers over and over again, making Him very real to me. I pray every day, and He's always in the back of my mind.

Q. *What would you say to the parents of children who are involved in the same behavior you were?*

Pablo: Listen to your kids. Then, really talk to them. Explain what your point of view is. And focus on the major problems. Parents sometimes focus on such small things they don't have any ammunition left when something really big happens.

Brianna: Wake up! I would definitely tell them to be with their kids, talk to them, try to get to know them. Help them out or get them help. If they are going to counseling, go with them. Give them some attention.

Jamal: Get closer to your kids. Be involved in their lives.

Sherry: Don't tell them what they can and can't do. Try to put the idea in their head and let them think they thought of it. If you tell them they can't do something, that's the first thing they will do in rebellion. Try to be their friend as well as their parent.

Q. *Is there anything you want to add?*

Brianna: Just that a family needs to spend more quality time together. I think most kids go through a time when they party and stuff, but quality time would probably help.

Sherry: Be totally involved in what they do. Know where they are, how they get to and from school, who their friends are, and who their friends' parents are.

Q. *What are your hopes and dreams now?*

Pablo: To really make a difference in kids' lives. I'm helping here at the drop-in center and trying to be a good influence on these kids.

Brianna: To go to school and maybe be a probation officer, mostly for kids. I really want to help kids because I know what they are going through.

Jamal: To be a good parent. Maybe find a job.

Sherry: To finish college and get a good job. I want to be a good parent and make sure my daughter goes to church. Eventually I want to help pregnant women who use drugs.

If there's anything we can learn from listening to these people, it's to get involved in our children's lives. We need to show our children love and understanding, and we need to be consistent. Although we want our children to "change" right now, we need to be patient. Remember as we pray for our children that God doesn't want to lose your child.

■ ■ ■

1. What risk factors are present in your situation?

2. How can you get involved in your child's life this week?

3. What changes can you make to reduce the stress of peer pressure or risk factors in your child's life?

PRAYER TO PRAY

Lord, there are so many pressures on my child, so many strong influences that are cause for concern. I ask for Your intervening strength to combat those pressures. Help me to do all I can to help lessen the risk factors. Help me to really listen to my child and open my eyes to what is actually happening in his/her life. I seek Your wisdom to make whatever positive changes are possible to create a better life for my child and our family. Amen.

PROMISE TO CLAIM

"The Lord is not slow in keeping his promise,
as some understand slowness. He is patient
with you, not wanting anyone to perish,
but everyone to come to repentance."
(II Peter 3:9)

Chapter Four

SOMEONE TO BLAME

Don't look for me," the note said. "I'm not going to tell you where I am." Carol read the hastily scribbled message again and again, but it never changed. Slowly the truth sank in. Debbie, her teenaged daughter, was gone.

"I thought things were going a little better," Carol told me. "We had tried so hard to salvage this relationship, but the problem had been going on for quite a while. It began in Debbie's sophomore year in high school. Debbie wanted to be in the elite group and finally pledged to a girls' social club.

"The night they came to tell her she'd been accepted, I could smell the alcohol as the girls sang, 'We want you, Debbie.' The smell was overpowering."

Carol paused, deep in thought. "After that, things changed very quickly. Debbie started becoming secretive and had a problem telling the truth. Then her grades began to slide."

Typically, Debbie's choice to run away was the finale of many months of strife in the family's home. The late-night sessions of escalating anger often ended with Debbie screaming, "You can't tell me what to do…I'm an adult now!"

Debbie's need to control her own life drowned out the sound advice of her parents to "think about your schooling, the future, the effects of your actions." The fire of contention was continually fueled by an older friend who had already moved out of her home. Finally, in the spring of her sixteenth year, Debbie scrawled the note and disappeared.

THE RUNAWAY PANIC

Every parent who holds that scrap of paper feels a gnawing in the gut. Disbelief, denial, shock, and emerging truth suck such parents into panic. In 1988, the last available national statistics showed that nearly half a million children under eighteen had left home without permission. Half return within two days, but about ten percent choose to remain away.

Most of the runaways go to the home of a friend or relative, and about one third of them will run away again. Most parents or caregivers usually know where the children have gone, and only about 40 percent report the runaway to the police.

When his son ran away, Jack felt confused. "I called the police immediately," Jack shook his head slowly, "but the officer only said, 'Kids do run away. Fill out this form and bring me a photo when you can.' It didn't make any sense. Why would my son even want to run away? We had given him a good home, a Christian upbringing and a loving family. All I wanted at that moment was to get my son alone and ask him 'Why?' But he was gone, and I didn't even know where to start looking."

It was a quiet day when my own personal volcano erupted. Panic overwhelmed me as I waited to pick my daughter up at school. As the school parking lot emptied, no familiar, jean-clad figure emerged. Finally I went inside to look for her, but the nearly vacant halls echoed as a final locker slammed and an unknown boy loped past me to catch the last bus.

We didn't even have a note from our daughter. She just disappeared. Her friends didn't seem to be concerned about her but rather were very secretive as we confronted each one. That let us know there was no foul play, but it didn't make her running away any easier to bear.

Finally, after weeks of hunting for her every day, everywhere we went, the authorities called to say we could see her. In a pictureless room with only one window, we waited, listening to a strangely pitched girl's voice outside in the hall. "I won't go home," the voice screeched. "You can't make me...I won't!" Then the door opened and a stranger with my daughter's eyes flopped in a chair in front of me. Detention-gray sweatpants hung on a gaunt girl I barely recognized, the outsized T-shirt knotted on one side. When had she traded in our little girl for this scraggled, defiant teenager?

Our daughter never came home again. Her only reason for running away was that she wanted "freedom and independence." At that time, the first reaction of the authorities was to place a runaway into a foster home. Now the authorities try to return as many children as possible into their own homes.

In the coming months we would learn of our daughter's involvement in substance abuse and the peer pressure to participate in activities that were totally foreign to my naive "Father Knows Best/The Waltons" family view. Years later we would recognize symptoms of genetic/birth problems that were unknown or undiagnosed at the time. Our daughter simply couldn't handle life on her own and followed the strongest influence at that time—peer pressure.

Unique problems come with "chosen" families. At the time we adopted our children, the psychological viewpoint was that environment overcame heredity. Now, of course, we know that isn't true. Although environment plays a strong role, heredity and birth defects cannot be ignored.

DETENTION—THE LEGAL HASSLE

On any given day there are at least 100,000 juveniles residing in a detention facility. In 1989, there were about three quarters of a million kids under eighteen who spent time in detention. The world of detention and foster homes often seem like a steel maze. Not only are we confused about which way to turn but we sometimes can't remember what the ultimate goal is. After we've slammed into enough legal brick walls, we begin to wonder why we are even trying.

It's difficult to remember that Jesus' words, "I was in prison and you came to visit me" (Matthew 25:36), apply to parents of rebellious children. Only God can give us the strength to walk through the blackened one-way-viewing doors of detention's lobby and sign in as a visitor. Only God can calm our voices as we stand face to face before our children, stare through a glass barrier into defiant eyes, and haltingly say, "Hello, son. How are you?"

WHERE DID WE GO WRONG?

It just doesn't seem fair. We've tried hard to raise our children right. We've loved them, we've worked with them, we've strived to teach them God's way, and we're rewarded with rebellious kids. Whatever happened to that Bible verse that says, "Train a child in the way he should go, and when he is old he will not turn from it" (Proverbs 22:6)? Oh, sure, maybe we made a few mistakes, but were they so bad we deserve this kind of treatment?

Some of these thoughts must have gone through the father's mind in the Bible story of the prodigal son. Although Jesus told the story as a parable (not a recounting of an actual happening, but a story with deep meaning), we can still go beneath the surface and relate appropriate feelings and emotions.

> *Jesus continued: "There was a man who had two sons. The younger one said to his father, 'Father, give me my share of the estate.' So he divided his property between them.*

> *"Not long after that, the younger son got together all he had, set off for a distant country and there squandered his wealth in wild living. After he had spent everything, there was a severe famine in that whole country, and he began to be in need. So he went and hired himself out to a citizen of that country, who sent him to his fields to feed pigs. He longed to fill his stomach with the pods that the pigs were eating, but no one gave him anything.*

> *"When he came to his senses, he said, 'How many of my father's hired men have food to spare,*

*and here I am starving to death! I will set out and go
back to my father and say to him: Father, I have
sinned against heaven and against you. I am no
longer worthy to be called your son; make me like one
of your hired men.' So he got up and went to his
father.*

*"But while he was still a long way off, his fa-
ther saw him and was filled with compassion for him;
he ran to his son, threw his arms around him and
kissed him.*

*"The son said to him, 'Father, I have sinned
against heaven and against you. I am no longer worthy to be called your son.'*

*"But the father said to his servants, 'Quick!
Bring the best robe and put it on him. Put a ring on
his finger and sandals on his feet. Bring the fattened
calf and kill it. Let's have a feast and celebrate. For
this son of mine was dead and is alive again; he was
lost and is found.' So they began to celebrate." (Luke
15:11-24)*

The word *prodigal* means "recklessly extravagant,
characterized by wasteful expenditure, lavish, one who
spends or gives lavishly and foolishly" (Webster). Not only
did this man's son recklessly spend his inheritance on lavish, wasteful living, but he foolishly wasted the relationship
with his parents and family.

POINTING THE FINGER

As we struggle through the rebellious, prodigal years
of our own children, we are painfully aware of the reckless

waste not only of money and time but also in lost and broken relationships. Because of the depth of this pain and loss, it becomes very easy for us to want to fix the blame on someone, anyone, or anything else.

"I think we lost Randy somewhere between the school and the court system," David said. "The school never notified us that he'd missed every day for two weeks. And," he added, "although he'd quit stealing from us, Randy finally got caught stealing from someone else. My personal opinion is that the court system stinks. You have to go time after time and wait and wait, then they read a piece of paper and say come back in three weeks, and you have to do it all again. I told the lawyer, if Randy can get punished for this first time and make it a deterrent and a bad experience, maybe he won't do it again. But the lawyer argued with me, and he got Randy off. Randy spent the weekend in detention watching movies." David shook his head. "Where's the punishment in that?"

David felt angry and hurt, betrayed by the authorities he had trusted. It's so easy to focus on these visible institutions and blame them for our children's actions.

"I wanted to scream, to hit someone," Heidi said. "My son couldn't have made this choice on his own. Someone else was responsible for this empty bed, this empty place at the table.

"It had to be his friends, probably his girlfriend, who influenced him against his family. She always wanted him to stay out later than we allowed; she told him we weren't being fair, that we were too strict. And now he's gone…I don't even know if he's alive. No one will tell me anything." Tears choked her voice. "His girlfriend says she hasn't seen him in weeks, but I think she's lying. If only he'd come home, I know we could work something out."

Heidi balled her fists in frustration. "Just where is God in all this? Why won't He show me where my son is or bring him home?"

Unless the prodigal child was kidnapped or was being abused—subjects far removed from what we are talking about (only three percent of runaways claim to have been sexually abused, and only one percent had been physically harmed)—it's important that we quit trying to blame someone else. The responsibility for our children's actions lies squarely on each child's own shoulders. Each child has made a deliberate decision to leave the security of his or her parents' home, to defy the rules of conduct the parents have established.

CALL ON GOD'S STRENGTH

Rather than lash out at others, we parents need to turn our thoughts and hearts toward God. God has not betrayed us or let us down. Rather, He is there as our rock and our strength to uphold us through this stressful, panic-filled time.

Isaiah 41:10 says, "So do not fear, for I am with you; do not be dismayed, for I am your God. I will strengthen you and help you; I will uphold you with my righteous right hand." We can claim God's promises because God never changes. He wants to be our strength, but we have to turn to Him and yield to Him. He can't do it as long as we struggle to handle everything on our own.

God is ready and waiting to undergird us when we feel as though we are sinking into quicksand. "The LORD is my rock, my fortress and my deliverer; my God is my rock, in whom I take refuge. He is my shield and the horn of my salvation, my stronghold" (Psalm 18:2).

It's easy to feel weak and wasted, as if everything is lost, but God wants to help us to get beyond that. Our strength comes through praising God. Even when we are seeing no results to the fruit of our labors—all the time, energy, and effort we've put into raising our children—the admonition of Scripture is to still praise the Lord.

> *Though the fig tree does not bud and there are no grapes on the vines, though the olive crop fails and the fields produce no food, though there are no sheep in the pen and no cattle in the stalls, yet I will rejoice in the LORD, I will be joyful in God my Savior. The Sovereign LORD is my strength; he makes my feet like the feet of a deer, he enables me to go on the heights (Habakkuk 3:17-19).*

In praise, God's strength is released so we can climb the mountain of court sessions, detention, and foster homes. God's strength allows us to calmly respond to our wayward children's accusations of "You don't love me! You hate me! I hate you!" God's strength, not ours, sustains us as we watch our children walk handcuffed through the iron gate and hear the gate slam behind them.

How much of God's strength did it take for the prodigal's father to wait and watch for his wayward son? It certainly wasn't by chance that the father saw his son "a long way off." The father had to have been standing at a lookout, shading his eyes against the distance day after day, to have been in the right spot at the right time. Following his example, we can use God's strength to be alert to the microbic turnings of our rebellious children. For every tiny shift our children make, we need to be ready to respond positively. It is the hope of those minute changes that keeps us from despair.

Again in Isaiah we find another promise to sustain us: "...but those who hope in the LORD will renew their strength. They will soar on wings like eagles; they will run and not grow weary, they will walk and not be faint" (40:31).

Each family represented in this chapter on running away said exactly the same thing about God: "He's my Rock." Carol, who waited nearly a year and a half before she heard any word from Debbie, said, "There's all this quicksand around you. You feel like you're drowning, and you need something to hang on to. The only thing I could hang on to was Scripture. I probably read my Bible more then than I had in a long time. I learned that there isn't anything that God can't work through. There isn't anything that He will allow you to go through that you can't deal with. It seems awful, nasty; but you can make it!"

FILL THE EMPTINESS WITH PRAISE

Although not every runaway child comes home, most eventually surface. When we see our children again we will have new problems to deal with (see Chapters 11 and 12). In the meantime, spending extra time with God can get us through the empty time. In our prayer time, we need to openly search out things for which we can praise God.

Do you know that your child is alive? Praise God for that knowledge. Not every parent has that assurance. The nauseating burden of not knowing haunts the waking hours of parents with prodigal children. It gnaws at their sleep and thwarts their attempts at living a normal, productive life.

Is your child in detention, prison, or foster care? Praise God that he or she has food and shelter. A recovering runaway told me she often didn't eat but scavenged food wherever she could. She sometimes slept in doorways and for a few days actually lived under a bed in her friend's home because the friend's parents didn't know she was there.

Do you have a friend or relative who is praying for you and with you? Praise God for that extra power. It means a lot to have the support of Christian family and friends. Just knowing someone else cares about you and your child will make your burden easier to bear.

Because communication with God is our source of strength, the more we read the Bible and pray, the greater our ability to survive. Spend some time every day reading a portion of Scripture. I love to search slowly through the Psalms, savoring the rich depths of David's knowledge of God. Substituting my own name in place of David's makes the Psalms much more personal. Take time this week to read Psalm 63; memorize it if you can. Those words that speak of God's upholding right hand and singing in the shadow of His wings can be very comforting.

It is never easy to live with a runaway, especially if the child is yo-yoing back and forth from the home. But God has promised to help us through all of our trials. Trust Him today for His strength.

■ ■ ■

1. In what way are you waiting and watching for the minute changes in your prodigal child?

2. How are you incorporating Bible reading and prayer into your daily routine?

3. Make a list of things for which you can praise God today. Call a Christian friend or relative and share your list with him or her so that you can both praise God.

PRAYER TO PRAY

Lord, it's been such a long time since my child rested comfortably in our nest. The empty place at the table, the empty bed scream at me every day and haunt my every breath. This is an agonizing time in my life, and I need Your strength. Help me to wait upon You for renewed strength. I choose to accept You as my rock, my fortress, and my deliverer. I praise You, Lord, because I know You care about me and my child. I praise You for the comforting support of other Christians and for the assurance You give me about the welfare of my child. Thank You that I can claim Your promises through these very troubled times. Amen.

PROMISE TO CLAIM

"God is our refuge and strength, an
ever present help in trouble."

(Psalm 46:1)

Chapter Five

SECOND CHANCE— FROM FAILURE TO FAITH

The first time she ran away, I thought my life was over," Rene said about her daughter Linda. "When she came back home, I could tell things were never going to be the same again. For about a week, Linda went to school every morning and came home at the right time, but I felt I couldn't trust her to tell me the truth about where she'd been. If I questioned her about her homework, she became belligerent and defensive. She wouldn't talk about her friends or classes. It was as though a void existed in Linda's life between the time she stepped into the school bus and the time she stomped to her room after school."

Rene watched the signs of failure begin all over again: lack of interest in school, reluctant interaction with other family members, a loss of appetite.

"My husband and I tried everything we knew to do, but nothing was working. When Linda finally dropped out of school, it really didn't come as a surprise. In fact, by then, school was among the least of our problems with her. She was failing life, and we felt like failures, too."

WE'LL TRY ANYTHING

The first time one of our children rebels, we are shocked, angry, and filled with panic. Most of us would like to treat the child as we would a misbehaving two-year-old. But all too soon we learn such tactics don't work. We attempt other methods, anything that sounds logical, and even a few things that don't show much promise, but we're willing to test them anyway.

Somewhere in the fogginess of our memories we recall not wanting to follow the rules our own parents set. Yet the intervening years have taught us that our parents weren't always wrong, and equally we weren't always right. There can be a mellow middle ground where each can live with the other in relative compatability.

So we try again, searching for some way to help our children past this difficult stage in their lives, to help them find that mellow middle ground. Not everything we try will be right. Sometimes we parents can be so focused on what we think is important that we miss what actually is important. We really want our kids to succeed. But when each new "second chance" is tried and fails, it's easy to become discouraged.

"It was like trying to fit a square peg into a round hole." Frank shrugged his shoulders as he spoke about his son Tony. "He just didn't seem to fit anywhere. We tried changing some of our rules, but there were basic ones we just couldn't give up."

Frank's wife Nita nodded in agreement.

"We insisted that Tony come home after school unless he had prearranged with us to go somewhere else. He had certain household chores to do daily. We wanted to meet his friends and know where they were going. His homework couldn't be put off until 'later.' He needed to be home by 10 p.m. on weeknights and midnight on weekends."

Nita ticked her list off on her fingers.

"None of these rules were unreasonable, but Tony refused to comply with any of them."

"We had to think of our other children, too." Nita was clearly disheartened. "If we changed the rules for Tony, those rules had to hold for the younger kids, too. It just wasn't working, no matter what we tried."

"When it was clear that he couldn't handle formal schooling, Nita tried to home school Tony," Frank continued, "but it was too hard to separate being the teacher all morning and then switching roles to being a parent at mealtimes and in the evening. Tony couldn't accept the authority."

"It was a real battle." Nita smiled grimly. "Tony was very stubborn. He could sit at the table for four hours and do nothing and then make up all these excuses why he hadn't done the homework…'the dog ate it,' 'it got wet.' We finally gave up the home schooling; it was just too much for all of us to deal with."

GOD WITH US

We feel such a sense of failure when we try so hard to work our problems out and get only negative results. Discouragement shoves us over the slippery edge of failure, and we begin to slide downhill to despair. In our own strength we cannot change the circumstances. This toboggan plunging down icy slopes toward hopelessness has no brakes.

But God doesn't want us to give up, to yield to hopelessness. We need to remember that although we may not be lifted out of this situation with our child, God is still with us. He can bring us safely to peace. In His strength and wisdom, every nuance of the course we're on comes under His calm control.

> But now, this is what the LORD says—he who created you, O Jacob, he who formed you, O Israel: "Fear not, for I have redeemed you; I have summoned you by name; you are mine. When you pass through the waters, I will be with you; and when you pass through the rivers, they will not sweep over you. When you walk through the fire, you will not be burned; the flames will not set you ablaze. For I am the LORD, your God, the Holy One of Israel, your Savior" (Isaiah 43:1-3a).

No matter how much we think we have failed, God is still with us! No matter how difficult the situation we are in, whether we feel like we are in a raging river or a blazing furnace, God has promised that we will not be overcome. We need only to allow him to sit in the controller's seat where we can lean against Him, yielding to His guiding choices.

It's so comforting to know that we can trust Him to get us through the prodigal years. When we feel that there is no hope, these verses can be a haven of comfort and security in the midst of the storm. God is not punishing us, nor has He abandoned us. Rather, He is our Savior and Redeemer who brings us through the storms of life.

When Linda once again slipped out of the house one night and dropped totally out of sight, Rene and her husband took their sense of failure to God.

"It is a humbling experience to say, 'God I can't do this anymore! I've tried and failed. Help me to allow You to take control.'"

Rene smiled, visibly relaxing for the first time in our interview.

"We are both very aware of God's will," Rene's husband added, "and both of us are patient and know that we need to wait and see why this is happening."

Rene nodded. "We may never see why. As much as I try, I still don't see all of it, but we both know God is there. We can trust Him."

It's nearly impossible to discern why each attempt to deal with our prodigal children fails. Neither can we understand just what causes our children to make choices that fail. But when we allow God to be in control of the situation, the results are fully in His hands.

Frank and Nita also agree on God's role. "God was our sustainer." Frank gripped his Bible firmly. "We'd get to the end of a particular rope with Tony, then we'd read the Bible and pray or go to church, and there'd be this special insight that would give us a new avenue to try."

"God is always there," Nita concurred. "If I had not had that Person to turn to, I wouldn't have made it! I literally wouldn't! There were times when Frank and I disagreed on what should be done, and the tension would build. A lot of times you just can't tell another person how rotten you feel. But with all we've been through with Tony, if I had not had God, I wouldn't have made it!"

God is the friend we desperately need in such severe times of crisis. Proverbs 17:17 says, "A friend loves at all times, and a brother is born for adversity." God is just that kind of friend and brother. He loves us when we feel rotten; He stands beside us when adversity would bulldoze us into the ground. When other people would leave us, God bonds like superglue. "...there is a friend who sticks closer than a brother" (Proverbs 18:24).

THE POWER OF PRAYER

When my own world was collapsing as I anguished over my daughter, I was so consumed with panic I spent less and less time in my daily devotions. Anxiety consumed my time and energy. Finally, my pastor confronted me. "Just how much time are you spending in Bible study and prayer every day?"

My lame response was, "Well, I'm not spending as much time with God as I know I should. But there is just so much to do. I can't seem to fit it in."

"That's the bottom line, Marcia," he gently chided. "You have to spend time with God first so He can help you. Anxiety does not come from God, and you cannot change your daughter's actions by worry. You'll waste a lot of energy worrying when God wants to give you calmness and peace. But you need to spend time with Him first in order to have His peace in your life."

I had to reevalute the way I spent my day. I needed to set aside some specific time to spend alone with God, reading my Bible and praying. It helped me to keep a prayer journal where each day I listed specific verses of Scripture I'd read that day and what they meant to me. Now I can look back into my journal and see the spiritual progress that turned my focus away from my anxiety and back onto God.

In our discouragement, anger, and sense of failure, we are not to give in to panic or anxiety. The apostle Paul, who faced many stressful situations that could have overwhelmed him, could have been filled with anxiety. But Paul urged the Christians at Philippi to trade their anxiety for God's peace:

> Do not be anxious about anything, but in everything, by prayer and petition, with thanks-giving, present your requests to God. And the peace of God, which transcends all understanding, will guard your hearts and your minds in Christ Jesus (Philippians 4:6-7).

God's peace is available to us but it isn't automatic. We have to present our requests to God. Through prayer we learn to rely on Him. In prayer we can tell Him all our feelings, fears, and hopes.

When we turn to Him and release our anxieties through prayer, He is free to fill us with His peace. Prayer is the key to peace of mind; it is also the greatest tool available to effect change in the lives of our children. When that second, third, fourth, or hundredth failure comes and we know there is nothing more we can do for our rebellious child, instead of giving in to despair or worry, we can continue to rely on the power of prayer.

Once we know we are right in our relationship with God, prayer becomes our most powerful and effective instrument. "The prayer of a righteous man is powerful and effective" (James 5:16). In fact, prayer is far more effective than anything else we can do.

Often in our bewilderment, we just don't know how to pray for our children. Maybe we don't even know where they are or what they are doing. But God doesn't leave us in the dark. He wants us to pray specifically. Instead of praying, "God bless my child" or "Take care of Francisco, wherever he is" or "Keep Susie safe," we can get much more detailed.

Using Scripture verses to give substance and form to our prayers can sometimes help when we don't know how else to pray. For example:

I will instruct you and teach you in the way you should go; I will counsel you and watch over you (Psalm 32:8).

Lord, please instruct Lisa and teach her the way she should go; counsel Lisa and watch over her.

Since you are my rock and my fortress, for the sake of your name lead and guide me. Free me from the trap that is set for me, for you are my refuge. Into your hands I commit my spirit (Psalm 31:3-5a).

Father, be Jason's rock and fortress; for the sake of Your name, lead and guide him. Free Jason from the many traps that are set for him, for You are the refuge he needs. Into Your hands I commit my son's spirit.

May the words of my mouth and the meditation of my heart be pleasing in your sight, O LORD, my Rock and my Redeemer (Psalm 19:14).

Jesus, help the words that come out of Donna's mouth and the meditations of her heart to be pleasing in Your sight today. Help her to remember that You can be her Rock and her Redeemer.

The heavens declare the glory of God; the skies proclaim the work of his hands. Day after day they pour forth speech; night after night they display knowledge....Their voice goes out into all the earth, their words to the ends of the world (Psalm 19:1-4).

Lord, I don't know where Andy is, and I know he won't go to church. But cause him to look up into the sky tonight and recognize the work of Your hands. May he hear Your voice day after day and night after night, never escaping the knowledge of Your glory, simply through the message of Your creation.

GOD HEARS OUR PRAYERS

The psalms are not the only source of prayer material, but their beauty, their eloquence, their depth of meaning make them a wonderful prayer frame. Although we may not immediately know the results of our prayers, we can always be assured that God hears us.

The thirty-fourth chapter of Psalms comforts us with this knowledge:

> *I sought the LORD,*
> *and he answered me;...(v. 4a)*

> *This poor man called,*
> *and the LORD heard him;... (v. 6a)*

> *The eyes of the LORD are*
> *on the righteous and his ears*
> *are attentive to their cry;... (v. 15)*

> *The righteous cry out,*
> *and the LORD hears them;... (v. 17a)*

Once we have poured our hearts out to God in prayer, we enter the waiting phase. Here we find that praise and thanksgiving are the fuel that keeps us going. It's so difficult to wait for God's answers, especially when we absolutely can't see any changes taking place. Praising God keeps our focus on Him. Again, the psalmist gives us an example to follow: "Praise be to the LORD, for he has heard my cry for mercy. The Lord is my strength and my shield; my heart trusts in him, and I am helped" (Psalm 28:6-7a).

Waiting for God to work reminds me of an astronaut away from the mother ship, floating solitarily in deep, black space. Dangling at the end of a tethered umbilical cord, the astronaut continues with the assigned work, all the while trusting the spaceship to keep life support abundantly flowing.

As we float in the black space of uncertainty concerning our children, hope is our umbilical cord anchoring us firmly to the Father's abundant, sustaining care. In hope, we can continue with our daily tasks, knowing we are securely bound to His inexhaustible life support: "We wait in hope for the LORD; he is our help and our shield. In him our hearts rejoice, for we trust in his holy name" (Psalm 33:20-21).

God is waiting for us to turn to Him for all our needs. He has not abandoned us or ignored our cries for help. Through prayer, we can go from failure to faith, from panic to peace: "Be strong and take heart, all you who hope in the LORD" (Psalm 31:24).

■ ■ ■

1. In what way have you been trying to work out your problems on your own? How can you change what you have been doing?

2. How much time are you spending daily in Bible study and prayer? How can you increase that amount of time to turn it into quality communication with God?

3. Make a list of some verses in Psalms that you can use as prayer frames for your child. If it helps, write out your prayers following the examples in this chapter.

PRAYER TO PRAY

Lord, I feel like I've tried everything and nothing seems to work. Discouragement and hopelessness have been creeping into my life, and I'm feeling a sense of panic. Help me to let go of my anxiety and trust You. Teach me to turn to You for hope and to not surrender to despair. Thank You for being my Friend. Thank You for Your strength and Your peace. Amen.

PROMISE TO CLAIM

"Before they call I will answer; while they are still speaking I will hear."

(Isaiah 65:24)

Chapter Six

WHERE DID I GO WRONG ?

I knew it was bad." Tomas stared out the window, focusing on his painful memories. "The police called about midnight and said that Miguel had been in an accident and they were coming to get us in a patrol car. My brother is a policeman, so we called him and asked his wife to come over and stay with the other kids. He had already heard it on their home scanner."

Tomas reached out and squeezed his wife's hand.

"I knew if they were coming to get us in a police car, it was really bad," Carmine added, lacing her fingers tightly in her husband's hand. "The terror and adrenaline and nausea that you feel are overwhelming."

Carmine twisted her wedding rings slowly as she spoke. "I'm a nurse at the hospital, so I knew everybody when we walked in the door. There were two boys on stretchers, and they were a mess. I looked at Miguel, and I knew he was gone. His heart was beating, but his eyes were gone; they looked like the eyes of a dead animal that you see in a ditch, all dry and glazed over... and I knew."

"The other boy looked worse," Tomas continued, his voice a bit huskier than when he'd first begun to speak, "although he was still alive. They took the other boy to the CAT scan first and said they'd work on Miguel later; so I knew."

"I said good-bye to him about thirty times." Carmine wiped away her fresh tears. "But I couldn't leave. I just couldn't go. I just kept thinking, Why did he get in that truck with a drunk driver? Why couldn't things have worked out better? Why did I mess up? Where did I go wrong?"

NEEDLESS SUFFERING

An overwhelming sense of guilt accompanies the prodigal years. For some people it is brief, a moment of questioning and then moving on to the next step. But for many others, the guilt hangs heavily on their hearts. It corkscrews into the depths of their souls, twisting and knotting, stabbing pain into every vivid memory.

Often the sense of guilt is self-inflicted. We believe that things would be different today if only we'd... "If only I'd driven him to the party myself." "If only I'd paid more attention to what she was doing." The list of 'if-only-I'd' phrases is endless, and the response is always painful. Every time we hurl those words into the air, they boomerang, taunting a hundred new and impossible scenarios, each a fresh torture of might-have-beens. Self-recriminating guilt boils in an angry cauldron, scalding us every time we stir the pot.

Not all accusations originate within our own minds. Many times other people are ready and willing to wound us with their cruel indictments.

"I felt a lot of guilt," Dana acknowledged. "I didn't deal with it well. Nothing that anybody said to me made any difference. I mentally flogged myself, I had done a bad job raising Wendy, and now she had committed what was to me the ultimate crime against our family—moving in with her boyfriend, rejecting our Christian values, and continuing to use drugs."

Anger still edged her voice. "But far worse than blaming myself was my mother pointing the finger at me. She came right out and said, 'What can you expect when you made mistakes yourself.' It was as though she were saying, 'You deserve this.'"

As much as we wish it weren't true, some people, even well-meaning ones, are all too anxious to rub guilt into our raw wounds. Our natural reaction to that kind of double pain is to lash out in anger at those who devastate us with their crushing tongue. Yet their words are no more damaging than our own. *Unnecessary* guilt is equally destructive regardless of its source.

This kind of guilt is suffered needlessly because it does not come from the Lord. No parents are guaranteed that even if they do everything right, their children won't go through this time of revolt. Even children who are raised within the walls of the church can rebel.

Eli and Samuel

The Old Testament provides us with two such examples. The priest Eli raised his sons in the temple. Yet I

Samuel 2:12 says, "Eli's sons were wicked men; they had no regard for the LORD." It would be easy to blame Eli and brand him with parental failure. But when he was given the child Samuel to raise (I Samuel 1 & 2), the results were different.

Yet when Samuel, a great man of God, who was reared in the temple, was an old man, the Bible says of his children, "But his sons did not walk in his ways" (I Samuel 8:3). Who was to blame for the actions of these wicked sons? Were their fathers evil or their mothers negligent? It becomes more and more evident that each child chooses for him or herself. The best environment, the best parenting in all the world, is no absolute guarantee that one's children will make the right choices.

The Bible doesn't tell us what personal pain Eli and Samuel experienced because of the actions of their children. But any parent is going to feel anguish when his or her children turn away from doing right.

WHO BEARS THE GUILT?

We often wrongfully force ourselves to bear the responsibility for our children's choices. When we are tempted to accept all the blame, we need to remember that God judges each person individually. Whether child or parent, each of us is held eternally accountable for our own actions:

> *The son will not share the guilt of the father, nor will the father share the guilt of the son. The righteousness of the righteous man will be credited to him, and the wickedness of the wicked will be charged against him (Ezekiel 18:20b).*

Guilt can be borne only by one person at a time. Each one is held accountable for only him or herself. That, of course, doesn't eliminate my obligation to be the best parent I can be, to try to help my children change from their rebellion.

GIVE IT UP

Dana recalled the moment she understood this guidance from God. "I remember being in the kitchen reading the Bible. This feeling washed over me of, 'It's okay. It's not your fault. You did everything that you could possibly do to help Wendy. The choice was not yours. The choice was hers, and she chose for herself...so...give it up!' It was a real healing."

The relief rang clear in her voice.

"I gave it to God. I said, 'Okay. If that's what You think, if that's what I'm supposed to feel, then I'm not going to hang on to this guilt any longer.' I felt released...free."

It isn't always this easy to release the sense of guilt. Many have to work at it every day, sometimes moment by moment. A year after their son was killed in a car accident, Tomas and Carmine were still working through the sense of guilt.

"The only way I deal with it," Carmine said, "is to just give it up, but it keeps coming back. I just pray again, and it helps for another few minutes."

God in His great mercy and love understands these overwhelming feelings of guilt. He understands, too, that we need to keep coming back to Him for relief. He is always there, waiting and ready to bear our burdens for us; He doesn't want us to collapse under the load: "Cast your cares on the LORD and he will sustain you; he will never let the righteous fall" (Psalm 55:22).

Even though we feel downcast and burdened for a time, we can trust that God will bring us through these painful prodigal years to a place where hope and peace and praise once again reign in our hearts. King David, who had several wayward children, experienced dark moments. He, too, turned to God for help: "Why are you downcast, O my soul? Why so disturbed within me? Put your hope in God, for I will yet praise him, my Savior and my God" (Psalm 42:11).

TORN RELATIONSHIPS

As the pain of the prodigal years increases, we find we are dealing with more than just our personal sense of guilt. As the load escalates, it sucks in other people. Both parents, whether they are currently married to each other or not, are snagged and flung into the angry sea of emotions. Siblings, the extended family, and friends are snared and left floundering, untrained for the shock of torn relationships.

The strain on the fabric of families can cause frayed edges and unraveled seams. We are so interwoven with one another that when one person rips away from the others, the continuity and strength of the family can be severely damaged.

We all react in our own way. Some withdraw, some turn to a friend, some become more united. People need to be extremely sensitive to the feelings, emotions, and pain of the people around them. The prodigal years can cause parents and families to bond more tightly or to be ripped apart.

"Louis didn't want to talk about it," Carol told me of the change in their marriage when Debbie ran away. "He just said, 'I don't want to hear about it! I don't want to talk about it! It's over and done!' But it wasn't over, and it wasn't done. Without my husband to talk to, I internalized a lot of it...until I developed an ulcer."

It can be easy to slip into depression, individually, as a couple, or even as a whole family. Having a prodigal child is very much like experiencing a death in the family. In fact, it is a type of death—the termination of family life as it was known.

Younger children may not comprehend what has happened. They may ask painful questions, possibly make unfounded accusations that slash at your heart. "Where is my brother?" "Why did you make my sister go away?" "He acts so strange I can't bring my friends home anymore. Why don't you do something to make him change?" Explanations often don't seem adequate.

"When Laura left home, my youngest son Peter asked for her all the time," Bill said. "He was only six, but he was really confused. 'When is Laura coming home? Will she be home for Christmas? Will she be home for my birthday?' I had to say, 'I don't know when she'll be home; I don't know where she is.'"

"I remember the first Christmas Debbie was gone," Carol reminisced. "We had a traditional Christmas party at my work where my boss played Santa Claus. When Santa asked my son Kevin, 'What do you want for Christmas?' Kevin replied, 'I'd like for my sister to come home.' But his request didn't stop with just Santa Claus. Many times in both private and family devotions, Debbie's name was first on Kevin's list to God. Kevin's reaction to Debbie's prodigal years really became the best example to follow...he prayed for her."

The changes in our other children can be a source of guilt for us, too. As their relationship with their prodigal sibling deteriorates, we may unnecessarily feel responsible for their reactions.

"Laura's actions embittered Andy, my older son," Bill said. "Andy became extremely protective of us. He wasn't going to let anybody hurt his Mom and Dad like that ever again. I think it's made him very cautious and very suspicious of people in general and definitely of close relationships."

BEAR WITH ONE ANOTHER IN LOVE

Just as each of us deals with death differently, so we each deal with the prodigal years differently. The guilt and depression may become so heavy that we need professional counseling (see Chapter 8). However, the Bible gives us some guidelines for living in harmony with one another. Christian sensitivity is the key. We must start with the fact that we are Christians, called out from the world by God as His chosen people. The same guidelines for living together with other Christians—the Body of Christ—apply to our own family.

> *I urge you to live a life worthy of the calling you have received. Be completely humble and gentle; be patient, bearing with one another in love. Make every effort to keep the unity of the Spirit through the bond of peace (Ephesians 4:1b-3).*

Bearing with one another in love covers just about everything. As the family members struggle individually with the death of their former relationship with the prodigal, they need to bear with one another in love.

GOD WAITS FOR US

The effects of the prodigal years can linger a long time, sometimes scarring many lives in the process. If we dwell on these effects, we can easily feel responsible for what has happened and take on the subsequent guilt. Although such an outcome may be troublesome, it doesn't need to defeat us. Instead, it can turn us to God.

The apostle Paul wrote, "We were under great pressure, far beyond our ability to endure,...But this happened that we might not rely on ourselves but on God,..." (II Corinthians 1:8b, 9b).

There were times, especially in the heat of a crisis, when I felt like I couldn't pray. In time I learned that was exactly what the enemy of my soul wanted me to believe—that God had left me to handle all this by myself. But God was simply waiting for me to turn to Him. In fact, He was very busy working behind the scenes away from my line of vision. I needed only to turn to Him and rely on Him for my eyes to be opened to the work He was doing on my behalf.

Pressure of any kind can become so great we are not able to endure it, but God is greater than any burden. When we are tempted to yield to pressure, whether it's guilt, defeat, despondency, or despair, we can be assured that we don't have to give in to it.

No temptation has seized you except what is common to man. And God is faithful; he will not let you be tempted beyond what you can bear. But when you are tempted, he will also provide a way out so that you can stand up under it (I Corinthians 10:13).

All of us have been tempted to give in to some form of guilt, defeat, or despair. This common reaction is not what God has planned for us. God is greater, stronger, more powerful than this temptation. Our job is to look for the way out, not blaming someone else or sidestepping our responsibility, but prayerfully seeking God's chosen course of action. God is the One who has provided the way. We need to allow Him to show us His best plan of action.

REAL GUILT—TRUE FORGIVENESS

For just a moment, let's consider real guilt. In most cases, the feeling of guilt is self-inflicted. But sometimes a situation exists that involves real guilt. Maybe someone really did do something wrong. How does that person deal with the guilt?

"I still have a hard time with a lot of it," Jim said. "I was really hard on Glen. Things weren't right in my life, and I took it out on my son. He tried to talk to me, but I just wouldn't listen. I made promises to him that I often didn't keep. I was always sorry later that I'd disappointed him. I could have done things so much differently, but I didn't, and now I'm paying the price."

When real guilt is involved, there is only one place to begin—at the foot of the cross. We must go to Jesus, confess our wrong, and seek His forgiveness: "If we confess our sins, he is faithful and just and will forgive us our sins and purify us from all unrighteousness" (I John 1:9). We may have to live with the consequences of our actions, but we no longer have to be mired in the quicksand of guilt. God is as good as His word. We are truly forgiven!

Confession and forgiveness involve more than just a moment in prayer. They mean feeling such remorse for our previous actions that we stop doing whatever was wrong. Some things are easy to change, others are not. The Bible says, "Fathers, do not exasperate your children...." (Ephesians 6:4a). Many major problems in the prodigal years began with basic exasperation. How can a child honor parents who are disobeying this command?

Many problems that need to be changed are not simple. They require in-depth counseling and even retraining (see Chapter 8). Whatever our former actions were, they need to be replaced with godly actions.

We may feel too weak, too guilty, for God to intervene and help us with these changes. But God loves us so
much that He has extended to us His grace, His unmerited
favor. We may not deserve His grace or feel that God should
help us, but He still covers us with the power of His love.

■ ■ ■

1. How have you been needlessly blaming yourself for
your child's actions?   Have you let go of the false guilt?

2. If you feel the pressure is too great to bear, what
can you do to seek God's guidance, God's plan of action for
your life, so that you can bear up under it?

3. What can you do to help mend the torn fabric of
your family?

4. In what way do you see God's grace at work in your
situation?

Prayer To Pray

Lord, I have felt so guilty, as though this were all my
fault. The pain of that burden has become more than I can

bear. I choose right now to confess to You any reason for real guilt and seek Your forgiveness. In addition, I give to You my burden of false guilt; I can't carry it anymore. Help me to rely on You, to allow Your power to be made perfect in my weakness. Amen.

PROMISE TO CLAIM

"My grace is sufficient for you,
for my power is made perfect in weakness."
(II Corinthians 12:9)

Chapter Seven

HIDING IN SHAME

I can remember standing outside in the hallway listening to the   familiar buzz of the downtown's businessmen's meeting in progress. I didn't want to go inside," José said, "but I knew I had to. The topic that day, presented by the local police department, was 'Preventing Burglaries.' The only problem was," and here his face began to redden, "the previous week my son had been caught burglarizing my next-door neighbor's business."

José's discomfort grew.

"My son had accessed my neighbor's store through an adjoining basement crawlspace while his friend waited outside in the alley. Fortunately, he triggered a silent alarm, and the police came in time to prevent any loss from my neighbor's business. But now I feel like I just can't hold up my head. It was bad enough having to go to the police station and all of the things that go along with that, but I have to do business in this small town." José shook his head. "And it's very hard for me to walk down the street, shake hands with my fellow businessmen, and know that my son was one of the burglars."

At that, Felicia, José's wife, nodded. "If we could, we'd move, but we can't afford to. The shame is almost more than either of us can bear." She twisted her fingers nervously. "I used to meet every Monday with a group of women, but I don't anymore. It just seems like everybody knows, and even though I shouldn't, I feel so guilty. I didn't burglarize that store, but I still feel responsible. I don't know when it will end."

FACING PEOPLE

When our children are involved in rebellious activity, the consequences of their actions affects so many people. One of our more difficult tasks is facing our neighbors and friends. Sometimes, depending on what the child has done, this is overwhelming, and we would rather hide in shame because of the embarrassment.

In our involvement in social clubs and other community activities, we see people every day. Especially in a small, closely knit community, the problem can mushroom out of all proportion to what has taken place. Many people respond by withdrawing from their family, their friends, and their business associates. It's easier to stay at home or stay out of the way than have to face other people. But withdrawing only increases the stress that we place on ourselves. Not only are we dealing with the problem that involves our child, but in our embarrassment, our isolating can result in our losing the support of our family and friends. We need to remember that it isn't so much *how* our family, friends, or associates can help us—it's their simply being there and standing beside us that often can help us to get through the most difficult times.

GOD IS OUR REFUGE

We cannot, of course, avoid the fact that there will be some problems and perhaps a sense of personal embarrassment in our community. Initially, a few people may pull away from us. There are always some people who will talk without having all the facts. When we have to deal with this, it is important to remember that our refuge is in God.

When circumstances seem to force us to retreat, a heaviness settles around our hearts. But God has a plan for us. He doesn't want us to feel as though we're wasting away or to lie awake all night groaning and crying from loneliness. He wants us to seek His presence:

> *How great is your goodness, which you have stored up for those who fear you, which you bestow in the sight of men on those who take refuge in you. In the shelter of your presence you hide them from the intrigues of men; in your dwelling you keep them safe from the accusing tongues (Psalm 31:19-20).*

It's the accusing tongues that shred our fragile ego. It takes only a word or two from a gossiping tongue to slice us into a billion fragments. How grateful we can be for the refuge that God provides for us. When faced with the accusing tongues, we can hide in the shelter of God's presence.

"I'm defensive with a lot more people than I used to be," said Vanetta, whose fourteen-year-old daughter was caught shoplifting. "A lot of people make judgements, not knowing what really happened." Vanetta fumbled with her purse straps, revealing her raw nerves. "Every time I enter that store, I always feel like the store clerks are talking about me because of my daughter."

The things that people say about us and our situation, whether they are actually true or not, hurt us deeply. Just knowing that we are being talked about wherever we go makes us want to withdraw. Turning to that shelter that God provides for us can give us solace from idle talk.

"I don't think my mother ever understood the real problem with my daughter," Vanetta went on. "She tried to make me feel that my second marriage was the root cause. Since she never accepted my second husband, we were already working with many strikes against us. I got to the point where I just didn't want to hear her say the same things over and over again. She really didn't understand the problem."

When we turn to God and ask Him to provide shelter from the accusing tongues, we may be very surprised at the source of that shelter. It may be a person, a place, or even a group of people. It may be simply some sort of change in attitude within ourselves. Whatever it is, we can trust God to shield us with His love.

"The people at work were very supportive which really surprised me because they were a pretty tough bunch," Vanetta continued. "The first person I confided in at work was a crusty old fellow at the next desk. Over our morning coffee he let me share with him daily. He didn't give me any advice; he just listened." Vanetta smiled softly. "That first day I burst into tears at my workstation, and two or three people went out of their way to offer comfort."

Vanetta twisted her coffee cup slowly back and forth. "I guess in the back of my mind I had the idea that

Christians didn't have bad things happen to them. I felt a sense of failure—I thought that because I was a Christian my family should have worked out better. But the people at work never said to me, 'You've proved that your religion doesn't work.'"

LOSING FACE

Although we don't talk about it much in our society, we do feel a sense of loss of face. Sometimes we find it very difficult to face other people when we have a prodigal child, especially if we have served in a position where people have looked up to us. We feel we have lost our credibility, and we may not be sure how to handle it.

A Sunday school teacher told me, "With my son in prison, I felt I no longer had the authority or right to be a Christian leader. Leaders, I thought, should be people whose family shows the results of 'doing it right,' and in my opinion, I had apparently failed somewhere!"

No matter how high our position of leadership, none of us is exempt. After his son had stolen a car, a pastor told me of his feelings of incompetence. "How could I stand in my pulpit and tell other people how to raise their children, how to be good parents, when my own son had caused such terrible problems. I felt like my authority was gone. I felt like I had nothing left to share with my congregation".

MAKING CHANGES

Like the firestorm of an atomic bomb, loss of face can totally decimate our sense of credibility. Blasted to our knees with our strength completely gone, we may feel that we have nothing left to give to other people. Isn't it wonderful to learn that when we are forced to our knees, we are in exactly the position we need to be in? When we're on our knees, God can work in us and bring the inner changes we need.

It's also on our knees that we can reach the very heart of God. Our natural reaction is to withdraw, to run away, to give up and say, "I can't be used anymore." But giving up and running away are not God's answer for us. God does not want us to withdraw. He doesn't want to destroy our usefulness. He wants to strengthen us and build us up so that we might be more effective for Him.

From our position of strength, on our knees, we can seek God's best way to use the situation. If there are things that we need to change, God wants us to be willing to listen to Him. Any changes we do need to make should be accomplished slowly, carefully thought through, prayerfully decided, and handled in a methodical, natural manner. If we have a regular job, we should keep it. This isn't the time to make an unnecessary job change.

If, however, we discover that what has happened will make a difference in our job, we need to take time to talk to those in authority over us. If possible, we should continue with our regular routines or social engagements.

Sharing our Situation

The people who are closest to us should be told that we are going through a difficult period. We need to be willing to open up and share with them. Being secretive puts up barriers between us and the people around us. Without some explanation, our suddenly unusual behavior can cause people to wonder what's going on in our lives. Consequently, people will react differently toward us. But if they know what's happening, they can be much more supportive.

We need to allow people to see our struggle. However, expressing our emotional pain should be done in a reasonable way. We mustn't dump on others, which could result in their feeling as bad as we feel. Our sharing, when handled graciously, will give people an opportunity to respond positively.

We should never publicly share the dirty laundry of our child or the situation. The damage that kind of information can do to our children and their reputation may be so great that they won't ever be able to return home and face the community or the church, even if they wanted to. We may create such devastation that our children can never again feel accepted in their hometown. The unrestrained recounting in public of our child's misdemeanors, whether slight or major, can completely destroy any hope the child might ever have of rebuilding his or her life. We can privately share the intimate details, such as in counseling or with a selected prayer partner. The Bible gives us a guideline for the type of sharing we can do:

> *Do not let any unwholesome talk come out of your mouths, but only what is helpful for building others up according to their needs, that it may benefit those who listen....Get rid of all bitterness, rage and anger, brawling and slander, along with every form of malice. Be kind and compassionate to one another, forgiving each other, just as in Christ God forgave you (Ephesians 4:29-32).*

If we do tell people what has happened to our child, we should do it kindly, without anger, and with compassion and a tender heart. We need to be careful that what we say will build up and not destroy our child. In that way, those who listen to us will hear the heart of God in the problem.

REACHING OUT

Each of us usually has an intimate circle of friends who know us better than anyone else. People who care about us and are willing to be supportive need to hear about our pain. We can go to them and tell them our problems and ask them to pray for us. They can provide a shelter from the cruel storm that is ravaging our lives. Most often this shelter is available to us within the body of Christ, especially within the circle of our closest Christian friends.

"I think my loss of credibility in the church was more apparent to me than was perceived by other people," Julie said. "That first week or two, I really didn't want to go to church or sing in the choir. When it was time for prayer at choir practice, it was hard for me to say to the other choir members, 'I need you to pray for my daughter and for my family because of our problem.' As time went on and the problem wasn't being resolved, I felt a sense of shame and embarrassment to have to go back week after week and tell them nothing had changed."

It's so important for us to remember that there is not a single Christian who has lived a perfect life. There is not a single Christian family who has not had problems at some time. All of us have had pain, and we will continue to have pain and problems as long as we live. We need one another to help us survive!

From that circle of intimate, supportive Christian friends, we may find someone who can sit beside us in church, someone who will fill that empty spot in the pew where our child used to sit. We may find someone at work or from our church family who can have lunch with us, share a coffee break, or accompany us on a long walk when we just need to get away from everything.

Picking up the shattered pieces of our lives can be difficult. But we need to return to a sense of normalcy in our everyday lives, to restore our regular routine of work and play. By reaching out to other people for support, whether in work or play, we can slowly start rebuilding, putting back together the broken pieces of our lives.

Julie was gratefully surprised by the reaction of her church family when she finally did have the courage to share her problem.

"The first week or two, I felt frantic, like, What am I going to do? What am I going to say? How am I going to face people? And then I found out that most people were not thinking that I had messed up. Several of the older women in the congregation came to me and put their arms around me and said, 'It's okay. God is strong, and He'll see you through.' I think it was their friendship that caused me to choose not to let this get me down or let it totally destroy my life."

We do not need to hide in shame from either our community, our extended family, or our church. Once we have reached out, our Christian witness can be even stronger as other people watch us trust God and rely on Him to see us through the prodigal years.

■ ■ ■

1. Whom can you contact to be a support person? If you can't think of anyone, ask God to bring someone into your life to be an encouraging, supportive friend.

2. How can you change the way you have been describing your child's actions and the entire situation so that there will be no damaged reputation to overcome?

3. What can you do to restore a sense of normalcy in your daily routine?

Prayer To Pray

God, thank You for providing in Yourself a shelter from accusing tongues. Help me to keep my focus on You and Your strength. As I face friends, family, community, church, and co-workers, may I show them the reality of being a Christian. Help me to be open to those people around me so they can see You at work in my life. Amen.

Promise To Claim

"Delight yourself in the LORD and he will
give you the desires of your heart."

(Psalm 37:4)

Chapter Eight

HELP!

"We talked with Miguel until we were blue in the face, but it didn't do any good." John shrugged his shoulders. "Maria couldn't handle him anymore, and we needed to do something."

"I thought he was at school," Maria nodded, "and then I found out he was running with a gang. When I told Miguel I knew what he was doing, he just sneered and said, 'Now that you know, I guess I don't need to hide it anymore.' He just didn't care...wouldn't listen to anything I said."

"We were at the end of our rope and the end of our patience," John added. "We needed some help, someone to tell us what we could do."

ADMITTING WE NEED HELP

There may come a time in the prodigal years when we recognize that we can no longer handle the situation by ourselves. It isn't enough to try to talk with our children, to reason with them, or attempt to control their actions. When we realize that the problem has escalated beyond our means to cope, we can admit we need help!

When we are so close to the problem, so emotionally involved, it becomes very difficult to be objective. With our cauldron of emotions boiling over, we have no way to step outside our problem and view it from a distance. We need the counsel of someone who can step back and see it from a different perspective.

It is not a sign of weakness to seek the counsel of others. Nor is it a sign of failure to admit that we need advice from someone else. The Scriptures admonish us to seek counsel:

The way of a fool seems right to him, but a wise man listens to advice (Proverbs 12:15).

Pride only breeds quarrels, but wisdom is found in those who take advice (Proverbs 13:10).

Plans fail for lack of counsel, but with many advisers they succeed (Proverbs 15:22).

Some of the greatest people in the Bible tried to deal with their problems alone and found themselves breaking under the pressure. Moses, one of the most well known, was in such a situation with the children of Israel. One day his father-in-law came to him and said, "Listen now to me and I will give you some advice, and may God be with you. You must be the people's representative before God and bring their disputes to him" (Exodus 18:19).

Moses listened to his father-in-law's advice, and the pressures of his situation eased. No matter who we are or what our position or our situation is, it doesn't hurt any of us to listen to the advice of others.

TYPES OF COUNSELING AVAILABLE

Many avenues are open to those seeking professional counseling. Often counselors—pastors, staff members, or lay leaders—are available at no charge through the church. Medical doctors may also provide counseling, as do mental health clinics. Many of these resources are also available at no charge, especially in some of the larger cities. Storefront clinics may offer medical and psychological counseling. Private agencies also offer counseling services (see Appendix), but usually their cost is relatively high.

It's important to remember that none of these sources on their own can change our children's actions. Our children have to make their own decisions to change. A counselor can only offer guidelines and suggestions, which can pave the way for possible change in both our actions as parents and the actions and attitudes of our children.

THE COUNSELING PROCESS

Once we've made contact with a counselor, we need to prepare ourselves for what will actually take place in counseling sessions. We should remind ourselves that our children are breaking away from our family circle and from family life as they have known it. Our children may do and say things simply for shock value to help sharpen the lines of the breakaway. They may even refuse to meet with us for group sessions so that we can't have an opportunity to talk with them face to face. Much of this depends on the type of counseling and the counselor handling the sessions.

It takes time to work through the process of counseling. No overnight miracles will take place. The process may go on for weeks or even months before we ever see any results. Our ultimate goal is the restored and improved relationship with our child. We also want our child to become socially responsible and acceptable.

At first, the sessions may be very grim, with accusations and emotions flying high. We will need to draw on God's strength to keep our own emotions on a mature level so that we are not reactive but rather are expressing calm and positive responses.

CHRISTIAN COUNSELING

If at all possible, we should seek Christian counseling in addition to any other type of counseling we are receiving. It's important to balance any secular counseling with sound, scriptural principles.

"My pastor was the best counselor I had," Zadell said. "I was having a tough time handling the sessions with the court-appointed counselor. I'm a new Christian, and I kept reacting out of old habits. I'd get really angry when my son would say or do something that upset me. Later when I would confide in him, my pastor would talk me through the problem. He always pointed to Scripture and showed me new ways to handle these old emotions."

Most of all, we need to seek the counsel of our Heavenly Father. Scripture says, "If any of you lack wisdom, he should ask God, who gives generously to all without finding fault, and it will be given to him" (James 1:5). Jesus is our greatest example for seeking the wisdom and the counsel of our heavenly Father. It was a deeply ingrained habit with him to often commune with God:

But Jesus often withdrew to lonely places and prayed (Luke 5:16).

One of those days Jesus went out to a mountainside to pray, and spent the night praying to God (Luke 6:12).

Very early in the morning, while it was still dark, Jesus got up, left the house and went off to a solitary place, where he prayed (Mark 1:35).

How God Helps

What will God do for us when we cry to Him for help? King David in the Old Testament often sought God's wisdom, crying to God from the depths of despair. He recorded for us his experiences of God's gracious responses to his cry for help.

I waited patiently for the LORD; he turned to me and heard my cry. He lifted me out of the slimy pit, out of the mud and mire; he set my feet on a rock and gave me a firm place to stand. He put a new song in my mouth, a hymn of praise to our God. Many will see and fear and put their trust in the LORD. Blessed is the man who makes the LORD his trust, who does not look to the proud,... (Psalm 40:1-4).

As we wait patiently for the Lord, we can be assured that He will hear our cry. The slimy, muddy pit of indecision, confusion, and uncertainty that causes us to sink can now be replaced by a God-given firm place to stand. As we turn to God and put our trust in the Lord, we can be assured that it is possible for Him to put a new song in our mouths, a hymn of praise to our God.

WHEN COUNSELING DOESN'T WORK

We will need God's strength and wisdom even more if the professional counseling we have sought does not produce the desired results. Sometimes no matter how hard we try, things don't turn out the way we had hoped.

"We started family counseling when Joshua was ten," Florice said, "but he wouldn't talk to the counselor. The counselor finally said, 'Just bag it, he won't talk to me.' She came in one day and said we were done. And we said, 'But you haven't worked with Joshua.' She just shook her head and said, 'I can't work with him; he won't let me, and I'm trying to teach you how to cope.' It made me realize that as difficult as the situation was, there were some ways to cope."

"One of the things we learned," Florice's husband LeRoy nodded, "was to just try to remain level emotionally and not blow. Because his problems were so severe, Joshua was not going to change. So if we had to tell him the same thing every day, we told him the same thing every day because he probably honestly didn't remember. That was hard for me to understand. It worked for me for a while to just tell him in a quiet voice. At the end, though, things just got out of hand."

"We were about ready to try some more intensive counseling by the time Joshua was sixteen," Florice continued. "But I was real skeptical because Joshua still wouldn't talk to counselors. I almost felt like we were pouring money down the drain."

"We begged his counselor to put him in a foster home, but it was so expensive," LeRoy shrugged. "We didn't have the money. We told Joshua, 'We love you, and we don't want you to go away.' But Joshua just couldn't deal with living here."

Florice added, "We thought about sending him to a Christian boys' home. He wanted out of our home more than anything, and that just blinded him to everything else. He wouldn't work with us."

Tears sprang to both parents' eyes. "Joshua ran away that day, took everything he had," LeRoy explained, wiping his eyes with a large white handkerchief. "It's been months now since we've seen him, and we have no idea where he went."

BENEFITS OF FAMILY COUNSELING

Counseling may address many side issues that beset a family with a prodigal child. Marriages that are heavily stressed can benefit from counseling at this time.

"My mother-in-law was so negative; I felt a lot of pressure and guilt from her. I guess I was the 'wicked stepmother,' and everything was supposed to be my fault." Martina still showed the strain in her voice although it had been nearly two years since Dominique had moved out of their home.

"Finally we had some counseling at community services because of a court order. The counselor met with several of our family members. When he met with me alone, he must have already seen the extended family attitude. The first thing he said to me was, 'You're not guilty.' I could have just hugged him, because I had really felt that this whole mess was my fault. What a relief!"

"When you're in the middle of this," Martina's husband Randy nodded, "you don't even think that there is anything out there that you can do. That's one of the things you just don't know about...the family services and the counselors. I never had had any experience with them."

"I kept a suitcase packed in the hall closet for probably three or four months," Martina added. "I was ready to get out of here, just take our baby daughter and leave. But it was our spiritual commitment to God as well as my commitment to Randy that kept me from doing that."

"It was the communication thing," Randy agreed. "We could talk about everything except Dominique. That was not resolved until we finally attended a marriage enrichment seminar. That seminar gave us the tools to allow us to work through the communication problem."

SPECIALIZED COUNSELING

Counseling may suggest some avenues of action that we have not considered before. If our prodigal child is involved in a particular difficulty, specialists in various areas can offer guidance.

"One of the smartest things we did," Martina continued, "was to contact the alcohol treatment center. It's a little bit difficult for those of us in the position we are in the community to go down and park our car in that parking lot where everyone can see it and will know why you are there. It really is. It shouldn't be, but it is."

"That guy was just wonderful," Randy said. "He was so sympathetic. He was the one who first talked to us seriously about codependency. We had never heard of that before. Some of the stuff we had muddled through on our own. We figured out, finally, after trial and error, some of the things we should do. He was the one who suggested that when Dominique was ready, we should try the treatment center."

Through prayer, counseling, and spiritual guidance, we can benefit from the wisdom of others.

■ ■ ■

1. Whom can you call for sound scriptural advice?

2. What counseling service do you need to contact today?

3. What do you need to change in order to follow through with the advice you've been given?

Prayer To Pray

Lord, I can't handle these problems by myself anymore. I need some help. Guide me today to a good Christian counselor and whatever other professional counseling I might need. Some of the advice I've been given seems so difficult to follow. Please help me to have the courage to carry out the suggested actions. Amen.

Promises To Claim

"Call to me and I will answer you and tell you great and unsearchable things you do not know."
(Jeremiah 33:3)
"For nothing will be impossible with God."
(Luke 1:37, NAS)

Chapter Nine

HANDLING REJECTION

The day finally came when I had to clean out my daughter's closet. I remember going up to her room—it had been empty for quite some time—and having to pull out all those dirty clothes that had been stuffed back in the corners. Shoes had to be straightened on the shelf and the dresser drawers cleaned. The emptiness and the loneliness were overwhelming. Tears streamed down my face as I pulled open the desk drawers and sorted papers. Things had been left alone far too long, and now the time had come for me to face reality: my child no longer lived in my home.

FACING REALITY

All of us at some point, whether or not our child is still living in our home, have to eventually face the reality of our child's rebellion. Maybe the child has run away, or perhaps we find ourselves having to say, "My child is selling drugs and I know what's going on," or "My child is involved in burglary, is an alcoholic, is a drug user. is a _____." Whatever it is, we have to eventually face the reality.

"When we learned my son was dealing drugs out of our house, I was devastated," Jerry said. "I knew there were problems, but I had no idea they were so severe. Jason had been abused at a very early age by his mother, my first wife. I never saw it happen, and I didn't learn about it until much, much later. It took place during those critical self-esteem forming years. By the time I had married Trish and Jason was living with us, it was too late. It had become such a deep-seated problem that my little bit of positive reinforcement didn't seem to alter anything too much."

A sense of rejection occurs as reality sets in. The children that we loved, cuddled, nurtured, and trained have turned their back on everything that we have tried to do for them. In essence, those children have rejected our life. That's the feeling we have. Someone we love has rejected us.

"Here Jason was being given many opportunities a lot of kids don't have for being outdoors, hunting and fishing, skiing and backpacking with his dad," Trish added. "Those things are normally helpful in developing one's self-esteem. Jason enjoyed those outings, but I don't think he and his dad ever got down and dealt with the deeper problem."

"Jason just seemed to reject all our efforts," Jerry concluded, "and reject us, too."

"I felt wounded and betrayed," said Carrie. "I felt like a total failure. I felt that nothing I had done from the time Zeke was born was of any value. That's a pretty strong way to feel. Just the fact that he picked up and left and didn't communicate, didn't choose to talk to us," Carrie continued, "only added fuel to the fire. I got to the place where I thought I was the worst human being on earth. It caused me to withdraw. Coping with rejection like that isn't easy."

FILLING THE VOID WITH THE TRUTH

We feel such a sense of loneliness and emptiness and pain when we finally face the reality of our children's rejection. In their younger years, our children brought such joy to us, and we remember those good times when they would run to us and say, "Come and see—come and do, be with me, Mommy and Daddy." Now that friendship, that companionship, and that joy are gone, and we are left with an aching void. "Where is my companion, my former friend, in my loneliness?" we cry. "Where is the balm for the wound of my heart's sick soul?" And the pain goes on! But how do we fill the emptiness? How do we ease the pain?

We are not, of course, the first people to bear the emptiness and the loneliness and the rejection, and we won't be the last. But we have a wonderful example in Christ, who tells us and shows us with His own life how we can bear these burdens. We can learn how to handle rejection by following Jesus' example. Jesus was rejected by the people closest to Him—His family, His church, His village. How did He treat those who rejected Him?

The book of Mark, Chapter 2, verses 3-11, tells the story of Jesus' healing the paralytic. Jesus was surrounded by people who should have accepted Him for who He was, but instead, the people were rejecting Him; they were making fun of Him. In essence, they were saying, "Who do you think you are that you can forget the Sabbath?" Jesus' reaction was to confront them with the truth. He looked right at them and knew what they were thinking. Then he simply said to the paralytic, "Your sins are forgiven. Take up your mat and walk," and the man was healed.

We can do just as Jesus did. When given opportunity, we can simply confront those who are rejecting us with the truth.

The second thing Christ did was to not give in to the people's demands. In the third chapter of Mark, verses 1-5, we read the story of Jesus' healing the man with the shriveled hand. The people who were rejecting Christ wanted Him to stop, but Jesus would not give in to their demands. Because it was the right thing to do, Jesus healed that shriveled hand in spite of the people's demands. If our prodigal child is making demands upon us that are contrary to God's law, contrary to what is right, we do not need to give in to the child's demands. We need to obey God.

"I called the police," Trish said about Jason. "We found the drugs in his room after our front window had been smashed. The whole thing was very frightening. The police came in and wrestled Jason to the floor and handcuffed him. Jason was screaming and yelling at me."

"We discovered he was bringing kids into the house while we were at work and he was supposed to be in school," Jerry explained. "We changed all the locks and didn't give him a key. I hated to do it, but it had to be done."

The third thing Christ did is recorded in Mark 3:5. Jesus was grieved and angry at the people's hardness of heart and at their unbelief. It's okay for us to be grieved at our prodigal children's hardness of heart. It's only natural to feel angry at their actions. When we are faced with right and wrong and somebody chooses wrong, we will have an emotional response: we will be grieved and angry.

The fourth thing Christ did was to persist with His own beliefs and activities when His family and friends tried to intervene. In Mark 3:20-35, we find Jesus' family thinking that Jesus was crazy. They were going to force Him to stop His religious activities and deny His beliefs that were so different from theirs.

When our prodigal children think that we are crazy to persist in our belief in God, when their values have changed and become different from ours, they may try to intervene and stop us. Sometimes very well meaning people who are not Christian may try to get us to give up our belief in God; they may say, "Where is your God when all of this is going on with your family? Why do you persist in believing in Jesus when your world around you is falling apart?" But it's up to us to keep our belief in God true and strong and to trust God for the ultimate outcome. We need to hold firmly onto God's hand.

The fifth thing Christ did was to speak in a way that would help those who didn't know what He was talking about to understand. He began talking to the people in parables.

Sometimes when we are trying so hard to present our Christian values to our prodigal children, we use hymns and phrases that have no meaning for them. We may need to change the way we talk. Stop and think about your children's life, about the people your children listen to, about the circle your children travel in, and try to relate Christian values in those terms. Although we don't use parables, we certainly can use words that are familiar to our children and that communicate a special significance to them.

The sixth thing Christ did to those people who were rejecting Him was to let them alone when they requested it.

Chapter 5 of Mark tells the story of Jesus' healing a demon-possessed man, a man who was demented and tortured in his mind and in his soul. When Jesus healed him, restoring him to his right mind, the people of the region begged Him to go away from them and let them alone. Jesus did just that. He climbed into the boat and left.

There may come a time in our children's life when we need to let them alone, to walk away from them. This may be when they are older, since when they are young, we still have legal responsibilities. But as we have talked about before, the prodigal years sometimes stretch into early adulthood and beyond. The time may finally come when it is best for us to walk away.

The seventh thing Christ did when people were rejecting Him was to continue to do His work even when people laughed at Him. Because of their rejection, Jesus wouldn't let them stay in the same room with Him while He was doing His work. In Mark 5:40, the people were laughing at Jesus as He was about to pray to restore the life of a child. Jesus said to them, "The child is not dead, but asleep." When the people laughed at Him, Jesus sent all of them out of the room except for those who were really involved. He then took the child by the hand and called her forth. He continued to work in spite of the people's rejection.

We may find the time in our lives when, as we confront our child and say, "Let me pray with you about this," that our child will laugh at us. That doesn't mean we are to stop praying. But it is a signal for us to go somewhere else to pray, to do the work of a Christian parent.

The eighth thing Christ did was to tell the people the truth even when they were offended. Mark 6:2-3 says, "When the Sabbath came, he began to teach in the synagogue, and many who heard Him were amazed. 'Where did this man get these things?' they asked. 'What's this wisdom that has been given him, that he even does miracles! Isn't this the carpenter? Isn't this Mary's son and the brother of James, Joseph, Judas and Simon? Aren't His sisters here with us?' And they took offense at Him." Jesus did not allow their offense to stop Him from telling the truth.

Our children may be offended at our spiritual stand. They may even be offended at our morals, at our everyday life values. But that doesn't mean that we should change them. We need to continue to hold our heads up and maintain our value system and our moral and spiritual stand. When our children come to us and ask us questions, we need to stand firm for what we believe.

We may need to back up our beliefs with Scripture, because our children are looking for a reason to rebel. We can never say to our children, "That's just the way I am" or "I believe it, and that's the way it is." We need to be ready to turn to the Bible and say, "This is why I believe what I do. This is why I take a stand for what I do." We need to stand for the truth even when our children are offended by it.

The ninth thing Christ did toward the people who were rejecting Him was to do what little he could, what little they would allow. Mark 6:5 says, "He could not do any miracles there, except lay his hands on a few sick people and heal them."

We may not be allowed to do a lot for our child, but we should do what we can, even if it is only a small thing. We need to try our best to do what we can.

The tenth and final thing that Christ did was to wonder at the people's unbelief. Mark 6:6 ends the passage with this: "And He was amazed at their lack of faith."

I can almost see Jesus standing there after He's healed a few people and He's just shaking His head in utter disbelief, utter amazement, at the lack of belief of the people who were around Him. We may feel just like Christ at that point. We may look at our children and say, "Why don't you understand? I've raised you and taught you and tried to give you the right moral values, and yet you still choose to walk your own way." It's not wrong for us to feel a sense of amazement at their unbelief, because Christ felt that way, too.

TURNING FRUSTRATION TO JOY

Often the source of our greatest pain is those who are closest to us. When a person close to us has chosen to walk away from us in whatever manner, we experience the deep pain of rejection and are left with feelings of frustration.

When we further feel the frustration of not being able to change a situation involving our loved ones, we feel as though we are up against a brick wall, and we feel unable to do anything to make it better.

"I came to the realization that there was nothing that I could do," Cliff said. "Absolutely nothing. I couldn't fix it. I hate conflict; I really do. When there is a conflict, I want to make it all better. When our son Sam continued to deal drugs no matter what we did to get him to stop, I felt absolutely frustrated. I felt helpless and full of despair. It's really a weird feeling. I always believed that I could take charge of my life. I had survived. I always felt that no matter how many times I was knocked down, I would just pick myself up, dust myself off, and do something else. But this time, I couldn't do that. I can't describe how emasculated I felt. Everything was totally out of my hands."

King David in the Bible, experiencing frustration similar to that of Cliff and of all of us who can't change a situation, lamented:

> *If an enemy were insulting me, I could endure it; if a foe were raising himself against me, I could hide from him. But it is you, a man like myself, my companion, my close friend, with whom I once enjoyed sweet fellowship as we walked with the throng at the house of God (Psalm 55:12-14).*

Another time, King David wrote, "Even my close friend, whom I trusted, he who shared my bread, has lifted up his heel against me" (Psalm 41:9).

Frustration is a grinding stone that wears at us day after day after day. How can we change our frustration to joy? Where is the oil of joy that will make the gears of our daily life turn smoothly without grating and jarring?

How dare we talk about joy when heartache and grief are sucking the very life blood away from us daily! And yet, we need joy to smooth our way. Joy is not a gift; it is not a natural happenstance; it is a choice. Joy is not related to people, places or circumstances. Rather, it comes from the Lord, who lives within us.

The apostle Paul wrote to the Philippians from his prison cell: "In all my prayers for all of you, I always pray with joy" (Philippians 1:4). Joy certainly did not come from Paul's circumstances, since Paul was in prison. His joy was not related to people, because the people Paul was writing to were far away. Rather, Paul's joy came from deep within his heart. Paul made the choice to be joyful.

I am sure Paul recalled the psalms when he thought about joy. Psalm 94:19 says, "When anxiety was great within me, your consolation brought joy to my soul." The consolation of God brings joy to our soul. Neither circumstances, nor places, nor people, but rather our relationship to God, gives us joy. In our sense of frustration and rejection, we need to turn to Christ and look for His consolation in our souls. At that point, we can choose the joy of the Lord in our relationship with Him.

Another choice for joy is to finish our grieving. Yes, we must grieve the rejection of our children, but we don't need to let our grieving continue indefinitely. There comes a time when we need to be finished with our grief and accept in its place the joy that God offers us.

Since our confidence does not lie in our prodigal child or even in the rest of our family, but our confidence lies in God, we can relax. As we choose joy, we can remember one thing for sure: God is in control. God is sovereign. All things are being brought together to God's greater glory.

LETTING GO

When we finally realize that we cannot change things, it is time to let go. Our awareness that it's time to let go may occur when God prompts us in our prayer time or other quiet times to let go. It may come during a counseling session when the counselor says, "It's time for you to let go. You need healing and restoration in your life, and you must let go."

Knowing that we need to let go and actually doing it, however, are two very distinct things. Letting go is a big decision, and it is difficult to do. There are several ways in which we can help ourselves to let go. We can write in a journal exactly what we are releasing. If our child is no longer living in our home, perhaps we are letting go of feeling personally responsible for our child's actions or decisions. Perhaps we are letting go of guilt, or we may be letting go of our frustration.

We can also let go of actions that have enabled our children to continue in their rebellion. Perhaps we have been supplying the money that they need for alcohol or other drugs. Perhaps we have been providing protection from legal involvement. Whatever we need to release we can write about in a journal. Then, on a daily basis, we can pray through our list. Consciously, openly, and even verbally, we can release each item to God. We can say, "Lord, I'm letting go today of the guilt that I have been carrying." "Today, Father, I am letting go of the frustration I have felt." We can also ask God to turn our hearts toward Him and away from the situation: "Restore to me the joy of your salvation and grant me a willing spirit, to sustain me" (Psalm 51:12). We can pray this prayer of David for ourselves. We can ask God to restore the joy of His salvation into our hearts and grant us a spirit that is willing to yield to Him.

Another tool for letting go of rejection and frustration is to recall happy memories when our children were younger. Recalling those good times, the fishing trips and the picnics, the holidays when things were good, can soften the edges of our hurt. Remembering our child's smile, bedtime prayers, and hugs will remind us that there were good times. The joy of those memories can ease the pain of our wounds.

One way to assure that this letting-go process is effective is to become accountable to someone else. We can begin by checking up on ourselves, going back through our list, and making sure we are no longer doing those things or bearing their burden. Next we need to decide to whom we will be accountable. We need to choose someone we trust, someone close to us—perhaps a prayer partner, spouse, or pastor. We need to ask the person to help us be certain we are no longer hanging on to those harmful behaviors. Eventually, as we become assured that we have, indeed, let go, we won't need to go through the list anymore.

GOD IS THE ANSWER

As long as we are holding tight to our frustrations and to our feelings of rejection, God cannot work His release in us. God is willing to change us. He is the answer to our emptiness and our loneliness and our pain of frustration and rejection. He fills our emptiness with Himself and His love. He is our companion and friend. He is the balm for our wounded soul. We need to allow God to make the changes in us that will bring about a new sense of personal acceptance.

With God's help we can accept ourselves where we are right now. As He creates in us that new sense of total acceptance, we will be able to relax with whatever situation we are in. We must not continue to browbeat ourselves or listen to negative people. With God's help we can draw around us people who will support and encourage us in our sense of personal acceptance.

The pain of rejection and the turmoil of frustration do not need to devastate us. We can experience the joy and emotional healing that God has for us. God will supply all of our needs according to his riches in glory (Philippians 4:19).

■ ■ ■

1. What do you need to do to face the reality of your situation?

2. In what way do you need to confront your prodigal child with the truth of his or her own situation?

3. Make a list of happy memories of your child and tell a friend about those happy memories today.

PRAYER TO PRAY

Heavenly Father, the pain of rejection has been eating into my soul. I feel so empty and so lonely that I just can't go on. I tried to change the situation, and I'm frustrated. It seems like there is nothing left for me to do. Lord, help me to let go, to release into Your hands all of my pain and frustration. And then, Father, would you help me to accept Your joy in place of that pain. Help me to dwell on the positive and the happy memories of my child. Thank you for Your words of encouragement to me today. Amen.

PROMISE TO CLAIM

" 'Though the mountains be shaken and the hills
be removed, yet my unfailing love for you will not be
shaken nor my covenant of peace be removed,'
says the LORD, who has compassion on you."

(Isaiah 54:10)

Chapter Ten

STEPS TO RECOVERY

I had to do something to change my routine. I was working full time, taking care of my family, including my father-
in-law, and cleaning our large old house." Carol talked
about the pivotal point in her recovery program. "I had to
make some changes. I think the Lord really helped to open
my mind to the idea that I really liked my job and that I
needed it. I loved my family, and I couldn't change who still
lived in my home, so I hired a housekeeper."

Carol felt boxed in by the rejection of her prodigal
daughter. "I had begun to resent all of it. As expensive as it
was and difficult for our family, it was still important for
me to do. It was a wonderful solution, because I had
reached the place where any spare minute was taken up

with grocery shopping or cleaning something or doing laundry."

Carol continued, "What a release! It allowed me to think of the more positive aspects of my life and that was good. I had time to read, to think, to go someplace with a friend. It helped my attitude, and it helped my family. I think when your attitude is really bad, your family just stays away from you. The change helped my relationship with my husband, because we had something else to talk about."

Learning to let go of the problems of the prodigal years is like being coughed up out of the center of a whirlpool. Although we are no longer caught in the center, we may still be riding the outer swirling edges, from which we have to escape. Since our lives have been so bound up in surviving the prodigal years that we have not focused on our own lives, we need to learn to renew and rebuild ourselves mentally, physically, emotionally, and spiritually.

MENTAL RENEWAL

Learning to renew ourselves mentally demands making a big change. We need to get involved in some kind of mental activity completely removed from our situation. Whatever it is, it needs to focus away from our prodigal child. One way is to learn a new skill. Is it time to learn how to operate a computer? Or perhaps you've never been able to knit. Maybe you've always wanted to build your own boat or learn how to tie flies for fishing.

Another way to mentally renew ourselves is through study. Pick a subject and take a community college course or a night school class—anything that would perk your interest. Or choose a new avenue of reading. This reading should not be just passive escapism; it should be something of substance. Have you had an interest in history? Pick up a book on Churchill. Perhaps your interest has been in antiques. Buy some books on a piece that intrigues you and study them deeply. And remember to spend more time in God's Word. Get a Life Application Bible or a Bible commentary or handbook and study it.

Another way to renew ourselves mentally is to deliberately change our thinking pattern. We need to replace our "I can't do this" attitude with "I can" thoughts. Every time we begin to think negatively, we need to deliberately stop, take a deep breath, and say, "How can I restate this more positively?"

Another choice is to deliberately change the people we associate with. If we have negative people around us, people who are always dragging us down, filling us with their problems, or pointing out our mistakes, we need to get away from them. We need to replace them with friends who are positive and supportive.

Some relationships may need to be deliberately walked away from simply to escape the negative influence. We need to be around people who encourage us, people who will help us to feel good about ourselves. We're not just looking for flattery, but we all have good points, and there are people who will point out those good points to us often. We really need to hear positive things.

Then, we need to create a mental picture of ourselves being happy, relaxed, and successful. We tend to become what we think. The adage "You are what you eat" is similarly true of our minds: we are what we think. If we picture ourselves succeeding in our families or in our jobs, we will try harder in both areas. If we picture ourselves as happy, our face will reflect our happy thoughts. If we picture ourselves as relaxed, our muscles will actually relax. All of these things will help us to build a new self-image.

Rebuilding Ourselves Physically

We need to rebuild ourselves physically as well, to make some changes that will cause us to physically feel better. We need to keep (or get) physically active. We can begin by developing good eating and sleeping habits. If we have only been snacking on fast foods or whatever happens to be handy and we're just napping and not getting a full good night's sleep, our bodies and our minds will reflect this kind of abuse. We may need to evaluate exactly what kind of foods we are eating. If we're eating too much sugar, we're going to bounce emotionally between highs and lows and experience a lot of fatigue. We need some good protein and carbohydrates, foods that will cause our bodies to function well.

If eating is a problem, take time to jot down for one whole day what you are eating and when you are eating it. If you're constantly snacking on junk food throughout the day, it's time to make a change. Our bodies need regular, nutritious meals each day that will give us the energy to function normally.

Going without sleep, having our sleep constantly interrupted, or getting sleep in snatches will drain us not only physically but also emotionally and mentally. We will feel tired and crotchety. It's important that we get a good seven to eight hours of sleep every night. Perhaps it's time to change some habits that will allow us to get that big chunk of sleep. Late-night television, reading, or other activities may need to be whittled down so we can get to sleep at a reasonable time. Spending fifteen minutes or so in quiet time with the Lord is a great prelude to sleep.

When we are physically rested and our bodies are restored, it's amazing the change in our mental outlook.

We'll be able to handle problems far more easily than we did before. Things that used to upset us will be more manageable.

Once we have changed our eating and sleeping habits for the better, we need to look at our daily physical activity. People require some sort of daily physical activity to keep their blood flowing through their body, and getting oxygen into their brain so that they can think more clearly. If you have been physically inactive, this isn't the time to jump into a full aerobics program. But it's easy to begin with a simple walk every morning. My husband and I currently take our dog for a walk every morning. A friend joins us along the way, and we chat about anything and everything while getting our exercise.

Later, if you're physically able, you can progress to jogging or running or to something more strenuous, such as aerobics or swimming. Exercise is a great release. We now know that physical activity produces endorphins, which give us a sense of well-being, which we need to effect good recovery both physically and mentally.

Some people may not be able to involve themselves in strenuous physical activity. But if the weather permits and it's at all possible, these people should try to at least go outside every day for a certain amount of time. Just getting a breath of fresh air, getting outside of those confining four walls, can offer a new outlook on life.

We can also change our daily routine just to give us something new to think about. Driving a different route home can be amazing. Choosing to eat out in a new place will break an old pattern. Even if we can't go out to eat, taking our meal to a different room can offer a new perspective. (Try sitting outside when the weather is good or go to a park.) See some animals; visit with some new people.

Anything that will change our behavior patterns will also give us a new outlook.

We definitely need to replace any negative patterns with positive ones. For example, if you have been isolating because you've been alone a lot and you haven't wanted to be around other people, it's time to break away from that aloneness and solitude and move out to be with other people. That can be accomplished by meeting in a group. Have lunch with two or three people. Get involved in a car pool. Whatever it takes, remove yourself from your solitude and move into a group of people who will replace that negative pattern.

Perhaps your habit has been to stay in a darkened room. Turn the lights on. Perhaps you have been involved in late-night television viewing or escapism reading. Both are very negative (I have yet to find an edifying late-night television program). Since there's a difference between light reading and escapism, be sure that your reading isn't replacing normal activities. Carefully evaluate your reading, and if you find that it is escapism, switch it to something uplifting. Make sure that it makes you feel positive about life and about yourself. (Again, read your Bible.)

EMOTIONAL RECOVERY

Because we may have been so stressed by the prodigal years that our emotions are frazzled, we need emotional recovery. We feel like we're walking on the ragged edge every moment. Counseling can be a very positive tool (refer to Chapter 8). Assuming any appropriate counseling has already taken place, we can do additional things to improve our emotional state.

One of the steps to recovering emotionally is to be willing to talk to someone else. The person should be someone who will understand what we are saying, someone who is emotionally stable and who will not divulge any secrets. The listener should also be wise and understanding, someone who cares very much about us.

When we are talking with this other person, we need to be open with him or her and not repress or internalize our emotions. It's important for our mental and emotional health to express what we are feeling. Once we get it out, we can talk about it, and we can then often deal with our problem in a new and better way.

Another emotional recovery step is socializing. Getting out with other people improves our outlook on life. As we interact with them, we hear what they are doing in their lives. We get new ideas, or at least fresh outlooks on old ideas, that we can think about. This causes us to become involved, and we aren't constantly focused on ourselves.

To socialize we can begin simply by joining a new group. The YMCA is a good place to meet other people. When starting a new hobby or renewing an old one, we can generally find a club of people who are involved in that hobby. Another way to socialize is to volunteer. Nursing homes and senior citizen centers always need volunteers. (My local newspaper prints a monthly list of organizations that need volunteer workers.) And don't forget your church. Perhaps you can join (or start) a Bible study group or get involved in some project at your church. Whatever the choice, we need to get out and be with other people.

Whenever we are involved with other people in positive interaction, our minds will help stablize our emotions. Whatever we choose to do, it should be something that will make us feel fulfilled, healthy, and successful.

GROWING SPIRITUALLY

Another aspect of recovery is our spiritual health. With all of the negative emotions, frustrations, and low self-esteem that we may have been experiencing through the prodigal years, we may have an impaired sense of our spiritual welfare. We may have felt that God didn't care about us or that we weren't valuable to Him. We may have felt that our prayers were not being answered. Maybe the words in the Bible seem to have been written so long ago they don't appear to apply to our lives today. That kind of outlook is a good indicator of spiritual ill health. We need to make our spiritual health strong and vibrant. When we are strong spiritually, we often can handle additional stress.

The first and most important thing we can do to regain our spiritual strength is to have daily personal, private devotions. Nothing is so important as starting out each day by talking to our Heavenly Father. In the quietness of those moments, we can pour out our feelings and our hurts and our hopes. We can open the Bible and read His words and let His spirit make those words come alive.

Devotions need to be daily. When we skip our devotional time, we lose something. All day long we'll have a sense of having to slug it out on our own. But when we have daily devotions with God, we know He's right there beside us. Having a strong daily relationship with God gives us a spiritual sense of well-being.

It's important that these devotions be personal and private. Only when we are alone with God can we reach the part of us that most needs healing. We need quiet, which is sometimes difficult to find in a very busy household. I became very creative in my own life. At times I had devotions in the bathroom, the only place where I could be alone for a few minutes! Other times I used the public library. I've even used my break time at work to find a quiet place to have private devotions. No matter where we do it, it's essential to our spiritual health to maintain our daily contact with God.

In addition to our daily personal and private devotions, we need to be involved in weekly group fellowship for spiritual feeding. Of course, this begins with attending the church or spiritual fellowship of our choice. The Bible says that we are not to neglect getting together with other believers: "Let us not give up meeting together, as some are in the habit of doing, but let us encourage one another— and all the more as you see the Day approaching" (Hebrews 10:25).

It's important to meet together with other believers to see what God is doing in their lives. We are encouraged and learn that if God can do that for them, He can work in our lives as well. Receiving outside spiritual feeding should be a top priority. It's best if this comes from a pastor, but a Bible leader or teacher can be just as encouraging.

We need to be sure in our group worship that the spiritual food we are being fed is solid. This is not a time for us to be involved in exploring extremes of any kind. To recover from the stress of the prodigal years, we need strong Bible-based teaching. We can measure the solidness of the spiritual food we are receiving alongside such well-known spiritual leaders as Billy Graham, Chuck Swindoll, and Charles Stanley.

In addition to joining in group worship, we need to be involved in group fellowship with people who get together for the purpose of spiritual interaction. The members of the group must respect one another as individuals. The group needs to accept you and offer open communication and interactive discussions. It needs to exhibit its trust in you.

The group shouldn't be one that draws you down but should be very supportive and enthusiastic. Each person within this circle should be allowed to grow as an individual, to make appropriate changes. Mental and spiritual stimulation helps the growth process.

BUILDING UP OUR SELF-IMAGE

Since success at anything necessitates a good sense of self, success in recovery requires our developing a positive self-image. If we are still maintaining a sense of drudgery and nose-to-the-grindstone and have no hope for our future, we need to change our negative self-image to one of personal worth.

Because building up our self-image begins with the encouragement of our associates, we need positive input from our church family, fellowship group, or other social contacts. It's important to be with people who will say and do positive things. With encouragement comes the building up of our confidence. If others see us as being okay, we probably are okay.

I remember as a child visiting my aunt and uncle's ranch in the mountains. There was a bubbling mountain stream with a log tossed across it. My brother ran across the log as fast as he could, stopped at the other side and yelled at me to join him so we could play under the trees.

When I looked at the water and that log, my heart started pounding, and I didn't think I could do it. But my brother just kept saying, "Come on, come on. I know you can do it." Over and over he encouraged me until finally with shakey legs I climbed onto the log and made my way across that "treacherous" mountain stream. The encouragement of those wonderful words, "Come on, you can do it," enabled me to finally succeed.

Encouragement is one of the most important things we can have in our lives when it comes to recovery. Encouragement continues to build our confidence. The more I heard those encouraging words from my brother, the greater my self-confidence grew. I reasoned that if he thought I could cross the stream, maybe I could.

Confidence gives us the courage to try something new, something better than what we've been experiencing. With confident courage we can risk extending our efforts and change our lives for the better. Courage gives us the strength to lift our feet and place that first foot tentatively on a log to cross a mountain stream.

Courage strengthens our self-image. It takes courage to make a change that will release us from the tension in our lives. It takes courage to look ahead and make some choices that will pull us away from the vortex of the prodigal years. It takes courage to keep trying.

Courage produces positive effort. We know that we are moving in a positive direction with the supportive affirmation of others. Positive effort produces accomplishment. Untried projects can leave us feeling negative about ourselves, but even just attempting a project can give us a feeling of accomplishment. The project doesn't have to be monumental. It can be as small as dusting a room or mowing the lawn. The point is to do it.

Accomplishment brings success. Nothing is so wonderful as trying to do something and seeing it happen the way we had planned. It may be just a simple task or a large complicated project, but that resulting knowledge of success is worth all of our efforts. Everyone wants to succeed at something. Of course, not all of our goals are the same, but we all need to feel a sense of accomplishment.

Accomplishment brings satisfaction. It feels fantastic to look at a completed, successful project and bask in the satisfying glow of accomplishment. The overall cycle from the very beginning to such a positive end builds our self-esteem, which gives us a running start to try again. Each time we attempt, complete, and succeed at a project, our self-esteem increases.

CHANGING OUR FOCUS

As our self-esteem grows, we can begin to reorient our lives away from the stress and strain of our prodigal children and the years involved with them and to focus on something new. Most of us have other family members besides the prodigal child. As part of our steps to recovery, we can focus on the other family members. Other children, our spouse, and extended family members have been through a lot of pain with us in these prodigal years, and they need encouragement, too. They need the love and attention that have been drained away from them by our focusing on the prodigal child.

"Mia's gone." Yolanda spoke of her daughter. "The last I heard she was traveling with a carnival and pregnant. I can't change that, but I can focus on the rest of my family. I've had to turn my focus on my husband, my son, and family members who live near us to remember that my life doesn't end with Mia. There are other things to do and be involved in. The rest of the family have increased in importance to me."

"It feels like we've been hibernating," said Max, "but I don't want to get involved in a lot of other things right now. RaeLynn and I have really been concentrating on our other kids, just spending a lot of time with them. We're trying to do some fun things. It seems like our son Lee would always get bad on the holidays. We used to visit my parents, and things would be so difficult. Now, we've been trying to create some pleasant memories."

Memories are tomorrow's treasures of today's experiences. If our treasure chest has been filled with discarded trash, it's time to clean out the treasure chest, toss all the trash away, scrub the chest down, and begin filling it with things of value. Whether it's a plate of a child's favorite freshly baked cookies or time spent listening to another person's hopes and dreams, the effort expended will produce memory treasures well worth keeping.

FILLING THE VOID

As we reorient ourselves to shift our lives away from the stress and strain of our prodigal child, we sometimes find a void that needs to be filled.

"I can see where people would turn to other things to sustain them. Alcohol, other drugs, illicit relationships, anything," said Arville. "They're reaching for anything that will replace this horrible feeling of emptiness. There is just a void. I filled it with being more involved in church, in getting very involved in local politics. I really got interested in the school board. In fact, I filed to run for the school board. It was something to occupy my time."

Being active is one way of dealing with this emptiness. With the confidence of growing in self-esteem, we can fill the void with our new goals as we reorient ourselves. But we don't want to get so involved in being busy that we forget that the best way to fill the void is with God. Recovery will not happen overnight, but we can begin by taking the first step today.

■ ■ ■

1. What behavior patterns can you change today that will give you a positive outlook on life?

2. What new hobby or activity can you begin that will help you build up your self-esteem?

3. What can you do today to create a positive memory treasure chest for your remaining family members?

PRAYER TO PRAY

Heavenly Father, it's time to make some changes in my life; I can't go on like this any longer. Help me to grow mentally, physically, emotionally, and spiritually. As I work through these areas of recovery, please help me to learn how to live a fuller life. I ask for Your guidance in reorienting myself and setting some new personal goals. Please help me to feel better about myself and spend some quality time with other people. Thank You for offering me the hope of positive growth in my life. Amen.

PROMISE TO CLAIM

"…those who hope in me will not be disappointed."
(Isaiah 49:23b)

Chapter Eleven

IT'S NEVER OVER!

I don't think about it that much anymore," Kim sighed. "I think about it at Christmas and her birthday. I determined that whenever I knew where Niki was, I would write to her. I wrote for about two years, but I never got an answer, even though my letters were never returned."

PLANNING FOR OUR FUTURE

Once our prodigal children turn eighteen or become emancipated, they do not automatically become stable, productive adults. The prodigal years are really never over. The time eventually comes when we have to plan for what's ahead of us. Some of those future years may be good. As our children mature there may come some wonderful moments of understanding and communication. But for some of our prodigal children, those years may become increasingly difficult. Just when we think things are going really well, they may take an unexpected turn for the worse.

"Things had been going really well with our son Ryan," Gayle acknowledged. "He'd had a job that ended well, leaving him with some money for the first time. He was feeling good about himself and had been away from alcohol for quite a while."

"It was then that Ryan decided to go to Bible college," Bob added. "He went in the fall, but something occurred during that winter that got Ryan back into drinking and really started him to spiral downward."

"He and a guy he had met at Bible college were doing some social drinking," Gayle continued. "Ryan felt like he had things under control. He didn't think he was addicted anymore."

"He didn't even know he was an alcoholic." Bob shook his head sadly. "We knew he had been involved with other drugs earlier, but this was the beginning of the end; he was on a downhill slide. He borrowed enough money to get through the next semester, but he ended up not going to college for some reason. He got an apartment and sort of looked for a job. Eventually he spent all the money, and because he was out of money, he decided to go back south, where he had been planting trees. That trip back south was the beginning of the really bad time. Everything began to snowball."

"And once again we had no contact with him," Gayle finished. "We later heard of a few places Ryan had been, but our contact was lost."

Even though we may not be in contact with our adult prodigal child, clues may come from the most unusual sources.

"As Ryan was doing all this traveling, even though we didn't know where he was, Bob and I were able to keep track of him because he was always ending up in a hospital for something. He'd give our address, and they'd send us all the bills. We never paid anything, because he was an adult," Gayle concluded, "but at least we knew where he'd been."

This kind of insecurity can draw us back into the turmoil of the prodigal years and prevent us from continuing with our own lives. We can choose whether to let it continue to drag us down or whether we can stabilize our lives so that we can go on.

When our child legally becomes an adult, we need to choose exactly how we are going to handle our future years. Basically we have two choices. The first is to continue responding every time our child calls in an emergency, doing exactly what that child wants us to do. Each time we think we are helping the child "just one more time." To continue in such a relationship is to remain in a state of denial and codependency. We need to eventually accept the fact that our child is now an adult and fully responsible for his or her own actions.

Our second choice is to give it to God.

"I prayed for Ryan every day," Bob said. "It wasn't a case of not being concerned, but we realized it was beyond our control, and I just had to turn it over to God. I could pray for Ryan, but that's all I could do at that point."

LETTING OUR CHILDREN GO

Releasing the burden of our prodigal children even when they are adults allows us to put our trust totally in God and to accept the hope that He offers to us: "To you, O Lord, I lift up my soul; in you I trust, O my God...show me your ways O Lord, teach me your paths; guide me in your truth and teach me, for you are God my Savior, and my hope is in you all day long" (Psalm 25:1,4, & 5). By doing this, we are allowing God to guide our future, releasing the sense of responsibility for our adult prodigal child.

Letting go of our children involves our choosing to allow them to live their own life. As they move into independence, they may make choices that can have disastrous consequences. However, those consequences then become their personal responsibility, not ours.

"When we came back from counseling," Gayle reminisced about a special two-week program they had participated in along with Ryan, "and he came back home to live with us, there were certain things that were set. We learned that we had to spell out exactly what we expected of him. Ryan was supposed to go out and find a job. He was not supposed to do any drinking at all. The counselors had told us not to overload him with rules, so those were the two we chose. He initially agreed, but later he decided to drink anyway."

"We prayed about this together," Bob said, "and decided what to do. Instead of just kicking him out the door, throwing his things in a suitcase and saying, 'Too bad, you blew it, you're out of here,' we rented him an apartment for a month. We moved him in, and he understood the rules. He knew he was going there because he hadn't kept the agreement. We said, 'We'll pay the rent for a month, and then you're on your own.'"

"He was supposed to attend AA every day," Bob continued. "But he wasn't following his 12-step program. If he had been making a strong effort at it, we would have gone a little further than that. He was attending meetings, but he wasn't trying to find a job."

BUILDING A BRIDGE TO INDEPENDENCE

It's important to help our children build a bridge to their independence. We don't want to just kick them out when they turn eighteen, but rather we want to assist them into a normal living situation. Although it isn't always possible, we can try. As in the preceding story, the parents knew the child could no longer stay in their home. They provided the bridge by renting an apartment for one month, explaining carefully the rules, and then backing off. Sometimes the backing off is the difficult part of this bridge, but it is the most important.

Renting an apartment for a month, of course, isn't the only way to build a bridge to our children's independence. Sometimes it's assisting them in finding a job. Other times our children don't want our help, and they simply need us to let go. When we do let go, we need to do it with a smile, which leaves the door open to a future relationship.

We need to make sure we tell them very clearly that we will always care about them. Because they are still involved in their prodigal activities, they may not want to hear about our emotional attachment to them. Nevertheless, it's important that we express our love and concern for them either verbally or in written form of some kind.

If they walk out the door in anger and we respond with an angry retort, it's like slamming the door shut and shoving two solid bolts fast into place. Neither one will be able to open that door again alone. Prying that door open again will take both parties and will be extremely difficult.

SEEING OUR CHILDREN IN A NEW WAY

This is also the time to adjust to a new view of our prodigal children when they become adults. We need to put away the childish image of them we have carried for so long. I clearly remember the day I looked at my daughter as an adult for the first time. At twenty years old, she was a wife and a mother and yet she was still living a prodigal life. I didn't like what she was doing, but I had to accept the fact that she was an adult and she did not fit the image I had projected of her. From the time she was a baby, I had created a pink-bubble image of what my daughter would become when she grew up, but her real life was totally different from that image.

Viewing our child as an adult can be something of a shock for us. One way to help this happen is to clearly state just who and what our child is now. And, if necessary, we may need to write it down, to make a list so that we know exactly who our child is.

"My daughter Angela is a dancer in a topless bar," said Aretha. "I hadn't heard from her in two months and didn't know what she was doing until a friend of mine saw her. Even though she is twenty-three years old and has every right to make her own choices, I still struggle with guilt. In some way I feel responsible for what she's doing. It's difficult for me to remember that I didn't make the choice for her."

Because it can be very difficult for us to adjust to a new view of our now adult prodigal children, we can treat them as though they were a stranger. We can ask ourselves, "If this were a stranger, how would I interact with this person in a positive way?" For Aretha to adjust to her new view of her daughter, she needs to ask herself, "If I were to meet a young woman who was a dancer in a topless bar, what would I say to her?"

ACCEPTING OUR CHILDREN

We may not approve of the lifestyle of our prodigal children, but we need to back off from any overwhelming negative emotional response to their choices. We did not make those choices, nor are we responsible for their consequences. If at all possible, we need to accept our adult children for who they are—just as they are.

It's so reassuring that God sees our children much more clearly than we ever could see them. If we could back off just for a moment and see our prodigal children the way God sees them, it might help us to more fully understand their situation.

First of all, God loves our children. That is the most important thing for us to remember. God loves our children more than even we do and wants only the best for our children. We need to remember that Jesus died for our children—our prodigal children—just as much as He died for each one of us. That's how much He loves our children.

Second, God views each of our prodigal children individually with a free will. Each child has a choice over his or her own actions, and each is responsible for the consequences of those choices. God will not force our prodigal children to return to Him. They must choose to return to Him on their own.

More than likely, because of their attitude and actions, our prodigal children will not listen to us when we speak truth to them. It's important that we remember that God has the responsibility for reaching our children with His truth in a way that each one of them can understand. Only God can make the truth plain enough to reach each individual heart.

Our adult prodigal children need to be accepted just as they are without our trying to change them. Our changing efforts are, actually, only manipulation once our children become adults. We may not approve of their choices or their actions, but we need to show them that we accept them unconditionally. They may never change by their own choice. Part of our own healing process comes once we recognize the possibility of their choosing not to change.

"After a while things went so far that I came to realize that Ryan was probably never going to recover. He had made a series of choices that eventually led him down the road to the point where recovery was not going to happen," Bob said. "I think God revealed that to me in a way, and I began to pray differently. I think there was a little bit of the healing process that began to occur there for me."

"It was like when you have a terminally ill person," Gayle agreed. "The grief process is taking place as you go along."

MAKING CHANGES

Change is a choice each person must make on his or her own. Sometimes that change comes through the maturing process. As our prodigal children grow older and see more of the world and life around them, they may come to realize that they need to change. No one can force them to change; they must make that choice on their own.

Again, our trying to force a change is actually manipulation on our part. I find it significant that the father of the prodigal son in the Bible did not send financial aid or haul his son out of bars or even out of the pigpen. The father allowed his son to remain where he was, suffering his own consequences. The father did not try to manipulate his son or force him to change. He simply let him alone.

MINISTERING TO
OUR PRODIGAL CHILDREN

We can minister to our own prodigal children right where they are. We can do what is morally right without being codependent. In the process of ministering to our prodigal children right where they are, we should take every opportunity to teach them without preaching. Many of them left our homes before receiving the full value of their growing-up years. They didn't have the opportunity to learn the skills that would help them to be productive adults.

We can use opportunities for teaching living skills to show our children how to do a particular task, but we need to remember not to do the task for them. For example, it's okay to show our children how to budget their monthly income, but they must be the ones to make the effort to keep that budget and pay their own bills.

We can also minister to them by offering them opportunities without forcing them to respond to the offer. These could be possibilities for employment or schooling. As adults, we know how effective and important networking can be in finding jobs. Our children, especially if they have lived difficult prodigal years, probably haven't developed networking skills. We can intercede for them with friends and potential employers and point them in the right direction.

The same is true for schooling. Our children may not yet have learned what types of schooling are available to young adults that will give them the skills they need for obtaining good employment. We can help them locate education opportunities.

Another form of ministering is taking that "cup of cold water" attitude. Whatever we do for our children, we do in the name of Jesus, not to enable them to continue in their prodigal activities but rather to show them the kindness of God's love. We have to differentiate between helping and enabling so that we make the right choices, choices that will minister to our prodigal children.

MINSTERING TO GRANDCHILDREN

Perhaps our adult prodigal childen have, by now, children of their own. If those children are caught in the activities that our prodigal children are involved in, we cannot allow those precious little ones to be punished. We can and should step in and do what is morally right. This may involve contacting the authorities, if necessary. If we find these innocent children suffering, it's important for us to take appropriate helpful, ministering action.

If our prodigal children do have children of their own, our role as grandparents becomes extremely important. There are some actions we can take to help those precious little grandchildren, the first of which is to teach them to know God.

If it's at all possible to be involved in the lives of our young grandchildren, we should step in. Our actions may be the only true source of stability and kindness and love that they know. We can have a lasting impact on them. In the moments that we are with them we can sing Christian songs. "Jesus Loves Me" is one of the best messages that can ever be taught to a child.

We can read simple Bible stories to them, depending on their age. We can play Bible games with them or even read Scripture to them, especially if they are older. Whatever we do to teach them about God and allow them to hear God's Word will be the most important thing that we do in their lives.

We need to be an example of God's love to those little children. Who knows, those little children may be the ones that will make the difference in our own prodigal children's attitudes and actions. If we are an example of God's love to our grandchildren, our own prodigal children will be able to see God's love in their children.

When it's appropriate, take your young grandchildren to church. I can remember taking my grandson to church with me even before he could walk. My daughter thought it was great to have a weekend morning free, but I knew I was beginning that very important early training for my grandchild. As my grandson grew, learned Bible verses, and took home his paperwork showing God's message, even in a childish form, I knew God's message was getting back into my prodigal child's home. I felt confident that God would honor my effort. He would honor the effort not only for my prodigal child but also for that precious grandson.

For a moment, let me talk to another set of grandparents—the grandparents of our prodigal children. Grandparents can be especially effective at this point in the prodigal child's life. They are usually a nonthreatening third party in the lives of all the people involved.

Grandparents can be effective just by being good listeners. They can hear the problems of the parents and listen to the prodigal children without being critical. Grandparents have the advantages of age, time, and wisdom, giving them a better perspective on the problems involved. Usually, when they give advice, other people can listen comfortably, knowing that the advice is not an emotional response but is solid and well tested.

Grandparents can be a good example to their prodigal grandchildren. As the prodigal grandchildren are testing new lines of thought and new avenues of action, they can come back time after time to visit their grandparents and find them never wavering from their solid Christian stand.

PRAYING FOR THE PRODIGAL CHILDREN

Although both being a good listener and being a good example are tremendous tools, our most effective weapon is to be a prayer warrior. The Bible says, "And pray in the spirit on all occasions with all kinds of prayers and requests. With this in mind, be alert and always keep on praying for all the saints" (Ephesians 6:18). Grandparents can join in the battle for their prodigal grandchildren by spending time in prayer at every opportunity.

Whether as grandparents or parents, we need to continue to pray for our prodigal children always. Instead of focusing on their prodigal activities, more realistically, we can focus on their needs as adults. Those things that are basic to a young adult, such as a good job, adequate housing, and a healthy family, will benefit by the prayers of both parents and grandparents.

"When Ryan first left school," Gayle said, "I knew he was in a really bad way. Yet at the same time I knew that there was still a possibility because of the spiritual element at work. I had some fairly good hopes. Inwardly I realized that the chance was slim, but any chance was worth pursuing."

Prayer gives us hope. Although things may not be looking really good right at a particular time, knowing God and His almighty power still gives us hope.

Prayer also helps us focus on God's attitudes towards us. God is our greatest example to follow in our attitudes toward our prodigal children. After all, we are God's prodigal children. What was God's attitude toward us while we were still in our prodigal state? Romans 5:8 says, "...but

God commendeth his love toward us in that while we were yet sinners, Christ died for us." God accepted each one of us right where we were.

By God's Grace

When we became Christians, all we had to do was first, confess our sins (1 John 1:9), and second, believe in the Lord Jesus (Acts 16:31). We did not have to wait until we were better or had changed or had done more good works (Ephesians 2:8,9).

Salvation was a gift to us of God's grace, His unmerited favor. As God's prodigal children, we certainly didn't deserve salvation, and there is no way we could have earned it (Titus 2:11, 3:5; Romans 5:15; Romans 11:6).

How wonderful to know that God kept extending His grace to us even when we didn't want it. If He treated us, His prodigal children, this way, how can we do less for our own prodigal children? We can follow God's example first by learning to accept our children just as they are. Second, we are to wait patiently in hope, never giving up. And, third, we are to keep on extending grace to our children even when they neither deserve nor want it.

God Is in Control

God is sovereign. We may not understand all that happens in our child's life, but God is still in control.

"I think that during the whole time of Ryan's prodigal years I never forgot about the sovereignty of God," Bob finished. "God knew exactly what was going on. He was in control. He proved that to me. When I would get into a situation with Ryan, sort of desperate to know what was going on, I'd always get some kind of answer. God kept reminding me that this wasn't an isolated situation; He was involved in it. The answer often came through events that couldn't be attributed to chance. It couldn't have been anything other than direct divine intervention. For me, these events were a direct message from God that taught me a lesson I never could escape from: we weren't out there doing it alone, God was actively involved!"

We would be utterly amazed if we knew all that God is doing in the background for our prodigal children. We are never alone in dealing with our children. God is always there. Sometimes we question God, and that's okay. We may never have all the answers, but we can relax knowing that God is still in control.

■ ■ ■

1. If your child is over 18, how can you help your child build a practical bridge to his or her independence?

2. In what way do you need to adjust to a more realistic view of your child?

3. In what way can you minister to your child right where he or she is?

PRAYER TO PRAY

Lord, it's difficult to change my view of my child. It seems like these prodigal years will never end. And now that my child is legally an adult, the problems are more complex. Help me to adjust my view of my child to one that is more realistic. Help me to minister to my child in practical ways that will show Your love. I want to follow Your example of extending grace to my child just as You did for me. Amen.

PROMISE TO CLAIM

"The LORD...will watch over your life;
the LORD will watch over your coming
and going both now and forevermore."

(Psalms 121:7,8)

Chapter Twelve

HEALING THE BROKEN RELATIONSHIP

My daughter sat at my desk writing thank you notes for all her lovely wedding gifts. Somehow the past two weeks seemed so unreal. From the moment she called and said, "I want to get married on Mother's Day," until ten days later when she stood at the altar vowing, "I do," there hadn't been time for me to reflect. Now, with the whirlwind behind us, I needed to regain some sort of perspective.

Where do I go from here? Do I let her trounce all over my heart again, knowing that she could easily crush me in this vulnerable state? Or should I keep a barrier between us that would protect my heart but would also hold her at arm's length until she proved herself worthy of my affection.

These past few days had caught me unawares and I was already trapped into letting my love show. In fact that first day when we shopped for a wedding dress my cautiously controlled love for her breached the barriers and overflowed. Her eyes melted as she twirled in front of the three-way mirror, but she hadn't wanted to ask. She knew she didn't deserve any special favors. Our glances met in the mirror, and we were mother and daughter again. "Do you want this one?" I asked. But the answer was already shining on her face. With a mother's heart I responded, catapulting into the sunshine again emotions that had long lay dormant.

THE NEED FOR HEALING

Broken relationships between parents and their prodigal children need to be mended and healed. When our children finally reach out to us, we experience an initial moment of panic followed by skepticism. Generally, we wonder what they really want. But if we are wise, we will look for opportunities to heal the relationship.

Both sides of the broken relationship need mending so that each can live a productive life. Parents need to experience the healing of the pain-wracked wound in their heart. Prodigal children need to fill the empty spot in their lives where their parents and other family members formerly dwelt.

TAKING THE FIRST STEP

Although we wish it could, the healing won't happen in an instant. The mending of the broken relationship may happen so gradually that both parties wake up one day and are surprised at how much reconstruction has actually taken place. At first, both will be very cautious. There's been pain and hurting on both sides, and no one wants to be hurt again. Our children don't know whether we will accept them, nor do we want to be stabbed again by rejection. Yet at some point, someone needs to take that very first cautious baby step toward rebuilding the relationship.

"I was so shocked when the telephone rang," Kayla said. "It had been over two years since I had heard from Jill. My first reaction was, 'What does she want this time?' Fortunately, I didn't say those words out loud." Kayla pulled a crumpled letter from her purse and handed it to me. "All she wanted was to hear my voice, to make sure I was still there. She talked for only a few minutes and said, 'I'll write you a letter tomorrow, Mom,' and hung up. This letter came in the mail about a week later and told what had happened in her life over these past two years. She'd been through a lot. That phone call and the letter marked the change in our relationship. It was a small beginning, but at least it was a beginning."

BEING OPEN AND POSITIVE

An attitude of openness is needed for the broken relationship to be mended. When no avenue of reconciliation is available, the relationship cannot be healed. It takes two sides to rebond that relationship; one person cannot do it on his or her own. If a prodigal child makes an effort to reestablish the relationship and the child is rebuffed and rejected, he or she will not continue to make the effort, and healing cannot take place. Had Kayla refused to talk to her daughter or thrown away that first letter, there could have been no beginning to restoring their broken relationship.

Nor is it possible for the parent alone to effect the change in the relationship to bring about full restoration. The parent can initiate the process but cannot complete it alone.

When a positive attitude exists toward rebuilding the broken relationship, the possibilities multiply infinitely. A casual conversation, a single word, or even a hug can be the beginning of change in the relationship. With a positive attitude, the turning point can come at any moment. It's important to make sure that our children know that we have a positive, open attitude toward them.

"We told Fidel he always had a place in our family," Manuel said. "Holidays are important to all of our family, and there was an empty spot that only he could fill. We made sure Fidel always knew when our family was getting together for whatever reason."

WATCHING FOR CHANGE

We all need to be alert to that first whisper of change, openly watching for that special moment. Change doesn't happen accidentally. It comes only after much preparation, part of which is our mental attitude. We need to be looking and be mentally prepared for the change that is about to take place. It's sometimes difficult for us to accept the fact that our prodigal children have learned a few lessons along the way, lessons that will have brought about changes in them. We need to be ready to accept an emerging adult, a much more mature person than the prodigal child who left our home years earlier.

Part of the effort involved in watching for change is to pave the way. This includes speaking positively to other people about our children. It's so easy for us to dwell on the negative aspects of our children's lives. We need to endeavor to speak positively, to find something good to tell other people about our child. It takes effort to look for the positive things, but like finding a diamond at the bottom of a gravel pit, it is worth all of our effort.

If we are openly watching for change, we will recognize that first sensitive approach from our prodigal child. Our first reaction is critical. If we react negatively, that vulnerable child, at a most fragile moment in his or her life, will feel rebuffed and may never try again. A positive reaction can make the way so much easier.

It may take a bit of practice on our part to be prepared with a positive reaction. When we're all alone in a quiet room, we can rehearse by looking in the mirror and saying some positive things. Having some praises ready to speak when that phone call comes, when the letter arrives or when we unexpectedly meet the child on the street can possibly mean the difference between permanent healing and the total disintegration of the relationship.

COURAGE TO CHANGE

It takes courage to risk making a change in the relationship. We may have built up the walls so thick around us to protect ourselves from pain that we're not willing to tear those walls down. It takes courage to begin removing the barrier between us and our prodigal children. We may make several false starts, but we need to keep trying. Remember, our children are just as vulnerable as we are. Since they won't have as much maturity as we have, we need to be the ones to continue making the effort, to continue reaching out to them.

Probably the best example we have to follow is that of the prodigal son's father:

But the father said to his servants, "Quick!
Bring the best robe and put it on him. Put a ring on

*his finger and sandals on his feet. Bring the fattened
calf and kill it. Let's have a feast and celebrate. For
this son of mine was dead and is alive again; he was
lost and is found." So they began to celebrate (Luke
15:22-24).*

He didn't say, "Okay, if you want to try being a ser-
vant here, go ahead. We'll see how it works out. You can
sleep in the barn, and I think your brother has some old
clothes you can wear. But don't expect to eat at the family
table."

Actually, the son would have been pleased to accept
such arrangements. After all, they were far better than what
he had just experienced. A barn and hand-me-downs
would have sounded a lot better than slop and a pigsty. But
the father expressed his forgiveness lavishly, joyfully, and
without restraint. We assume that the story had a happy
ending. We also assume that the father's trust was well
placed and that the son was truly repentant and did not
betray his family again.

In this case, the son did ask for forgiveness, acknowl-
edging his sin against both God and his family. It seems to
me, however, that the father hardly heard those words. Very
possibly the extravagant outpouring of his love for his son
started back on the road when the son was just a speck of
dust in the distance: "But while he was still a long way off,
his father saw him and was filled with compassion for him;
he ran to his son, threw his arms around him and kissed
him" (Luke 15:20).

That hug and the kiss weren't put off until the son
had cleaned up and put on proper clothes. The father did-
n't even wait until the son had come all the way home.
Instead, he ran to meet him. What courage!

It's so difficult to risk all those feelings again. That
father didn't know why his son was coming home. Maybe it

was to ask for more money and to leave again just as soon as he was cleaned up and had some food in his belly and cash in his pocket.

It took courage for that father to react positively to this first step of his son's change. And it takes courage for us to react in that same manner. Reaching out to our prodigal children with love, extending our acceptance, and offering forgiveness to them take an incredible amount of courage. Not many of us are willing to risk to that degree.

EXAMPLES OF JESUS' LOVE, ACCEPTANCE, AND FORGIVENESS

Love, acceptance, and forgiveness all sound nice on paper. But how can we actually put them into practice? As usual, we turn to Scripture for guidance. Only God can really tell us how to do it. We have the example of God's love on the cross:

> He was despised and rejected by men, a man of sorrows, and familiar with suffering. Like one from whom men hide their faces he was despised, and we esteemed him not. Surely he took up our infirmities and carried our sorrows, yet we considered him stricken by God, smitten by him, and afflicted. But he was pierced for our transgressions, he was crushed for our iniquities; the punishment that brought us peace was upon him, and by his wounds we are healed. We all, like sheep, have gone astray, each of us has turned to his own way; and the LORD has laid on him the iniquity of us all (Isaiah 53:3-6).

By choice, Christ committed an act of love through His death, knowing that many would reject and despise Him. In Matthew 5:46, we are confronted with this truth: "If you love those who love you, what reward will you get?"

Instead, Christ commands us to love our enemies and pray for those who persecute us (Matthew 5:44). Luke 6:29 adds, "If someone strikes you on one cheek, turn to him the other also. If someone takes your cloak, do not stop him from taking your tunic." God's love goes far beyond words.

An example of acceptance is shown in Christ's attitude toward the woman at the well (John 4:1-42). The woman knew that as a Jew, Jesus should not have said so much as a single word to her or asked anything of her. Yet, He accepted her just as she was, treated her as He treated everyone else. It wasn't only tradition that should have made Him keep his distance. She was truly a "fallen woman," and He really shouldn't have even been seen with her. I can just hear the tongues wagging, "It will taint His ministry, being seen with her." "People might get the wrong idea and think that Jesus condones her and the way she lives."

But far from condoning her lifestyle, Jesus confronted her with the reality of it and offered her something new, something better. But first He accepted her just as she was.

Along with these examples of undeserved love and undeserved acceptance, we find undeserved forgiveness. The woman caught in adultery (John 8:3-11) didn't deserve forgiveness. Jesus didn't make an example of her or cause her undue shame but rather asked a simple question that put everything into proper perspective:

"Woman, where are they? Has no one condemned you?"

"No one, sir," she said.

"Then neither do I condemn you," Jesus declared. "Go now and leave your life of sin." (John 8:10-11)

The woman didn't ask for forgiveness, but Jesus gave it to her without her asking. He treated her in a one-on-one situation exactly the way His Father had treated the stubborn, rebellious, prodigal people of Israel. Without their asking for forgiveness, He offered it anyway: "I will heal their waywardness and love them freely, for my anger has turned away from them" (Hosea 14:4).

We also need to forgive even before we're asked: "And when you stand praying, if you hold anything against anyone, forgive him, so that your Father in heaven may forgive you your sins" (Mark 11:25). Forgiveness must begin within our own heart before we can extend it our prodigal children. If we have already forgiven them while we were on our knees, we will be ready to display that forgiveness openly when they come to us.

SOWING THE SEEDS OF LOVE, ACCEPTANCE, AND FORGIVENESS

Love, acceptance, and forgiveness are the foundation on which we can rebuild our relationship. But how do we sow the seeds of love, acceptance, and forgiveness? We need first to be willing to extend love, acceptance, and forgiveness. No matter how many times our prodigal children make that false start and try again, we need to be willing to meet them right where they are: "If your brother sins, rebuke him, and if he repents, forgive him. If he sins against you seven times in a day, and seven times comes back to you and says, 'I repent,' forgive him" (Luke 17:3,4).

More than just saying words of love or acceptance or forgiveness, we need to back them up with our actions: "Dear children, let us not love with words or tongue but with actions and in truth" (1 John 3:18).

Our actions can take many avenues of expression. Providing a special wedding dress for my daughter was just the beginning of my sowing those seeds of love and acceptance. Another avenue of expression came with the actual wedding itself. Instead of having a small, family-only ceremony, I invited some of our personal friends, people who had been special to our daughter, as well as some of her current friends. There wasn't time to create an extravangaza, which would have been totally out of place, but with a little help from my friends, we provided a pleasant, memorable wedding.

Probably the most visible way of sowing those seeds of love, acceptance, and forgiveness will come in providing pain-free, noncritical moments of interaction with our prodigal children. It's often the little things in life that make the greatest impression. Just as a seed is tiny and yet will eventually produce a flower or even a towering tree, so these moments may be tiny. Such a simple thing as writing a positive letter without criticism or making a relaxed phone call is a small seed easy to sow. A casual invitation, such as, "Will you meet me for a cup of coffee?", can be the seed from which a whole new relationship will grow. If the prodigal child is now an adult and has a family, why not drop in with a gift, perhaps for a new baby. The gift need not be expensive, nor does it need to be for a special occasion; it just needs to be a gift of love. Send a photo of a fun memory. Take time to go through the family photo album and have duplicates made of old photographs so that your child can have his or her own copies.

CULTIVATING THE NEW RELATIONSHIP

Just as a gardener shapes a garden so can we shape and cultivate our new relationship with our child. A professional gardener will spend many, many hours planning the garden he or she hopes to grow, and we should do no differently. We need to very thoughtfully and wisely choose to shape and form what we want for our new relationship.

Not only is there shape and form to the relationship, but there's color as well. Whether pale or vivid, color is brought about by our attitude. The beauty of our new relationship is brilliantly displayed through our attitude toward our prodigal child. A vibrant color can be planted by showing our children how much we really value them by affirming them as adults.

Our children need to know that as they have passed from childhood into adulthood, we accept them as adults. If they have been away from our home, they may have missed out on some of the family traditions that would have marked their passage into adulthood. If possible, we can identify those special family traditions and reenact them in some manner.

Although each family is different, quite often a wedding marks the move into adulthood, as does graduation from school or some other special event. Even if the event has actually passed, a family dinner or gathering with the prodigal child as the honoree could in some way make up for that missed rite of passage.

Rebuilding a relationship takes time and effort, thought and care. The relationship cannot grow without watering and weeding, but the results are worth the time and effort put into it. Part of our time and effort can be shown through increasing opportunities for interaction. As the garden grows, we can deepen the work that we do and provide more opportunities for interaction.

The more opportunities we provide for interaction with our child, the more we will be exposing our true self to our prodigal child. This is a time to stand firm as a Christian. Most of all, the strong foundation of this renewed relationship must be God.   In an effort to bridge the relationship, we should be careful not to compromise our Christianity. Although, we want to accept our children and draw them back into the family fold, we should in no way condone any continued antisocial behavior.

Without preaching at them, we need to positively affirm our position in Christ. We can do this in a number of ways. For example, giving them a simple hug and saying, "I really love you, and I've been praying for you," will gently remind them that we are still the strong Christians that they knew when they were young.

CHRISTIAN FRIENDSHIP

My friends...they were another risk. How would they view my actions? Would they pity me or think I was foolish to go to so much trouble for a prodigal child? Would they turn their backs on me?

Christian friends, I've learned, are the greatest people on earth! As soon as the news about my daughter's wedding was out, my friends converged—all with the same question: "How can I help?" Nearly all of them said they wanted to express some tangible love to our daughter. It was my Christian friends who stepped in to coordinate the wedding and make floral arrangements and a bridal bouquet. They took pictures and created a reception complete with tiered cake and delicious punch. They loaned silver sets and cleaned up when it was all over. Others took over my regular responsibilities so that I could be free to concentrate on just the wedding. What a magnificent expression of God's love—love in action!

PRAY FOR OUR CHILDREN

Because the years ahead are not going to be easy for our children, we need to keep on praying for them. There may still be some residual effects of their prodigal years that cannot be erased. Because our children may have to pay a very high price for their prodigal behavior, they will need our continued prayer. Our task of praying for our children never diminishes. We need to keep on being strong prayer warriors on their behalf.

■ ■ ■

1. What can you do to prepare the way for rebuilding the broken relationship?

2. How can you openly watch for change, and what effort do you need to make?

3. What can you do this week to plant seeds of love, acceptance, and forgiveness?

Prayer To Pray

Lord, I've waited and watched for a long time, and I'm ready for this broken relationship to be mended. Show me, God, how I can sow those seeds of love, acceptance, and forgiveness. Give me the courage I will need to risk change. Show me what I can do to bring about that change. If there are things that I am still holding against my prodigal child, I ask for Your forgiveness. Help me to forgive my child.

Thank You for new beginnings. Thank You for the opportunity to start over again. Amen.

PROMISE TO CLAIM

"I have seen his ways, but I will heal him;
I will guide him and restore comfort to him,
creating praise on the lips of the mourners in Israel."
(Isaiah 57:18-19)

Chapter Thirteen

REACHING OUT TO OTHERS

I t's amazing how many people in this world are hurting. No one is excluded," Carol said. "I thought my experience wouldn't be worth discussing with anybody else. I never volunteered any information, but the Lord seemed to put me in the right place, and the people who were facing similar problems with their kids asked the right questions."

TAKING A RISK

A giant pain accompanies the risk of telling the truth about our experiences during the prodigal years. Too many people hide their pain; they don't want people to know the truth. They may have many reasons for hiding the truth. Perhaps it's embarassment. Perhaps it's a natural reticence

165

to talk about their personal life. But whatever the reason, it is important for us to risk that pain of telling the truth.

Although we don't need to talk about it constantly, and we certainly shouldn't discuss it at inappropriate times, in inappropriate places, and with inappropriate people, we need to be graciously open and honest with our experience. Joyce Clark wrote a poem about her feelings during her son's prodigal years:

I Think of You Only Now and Then

I think of you only now and then...only when...
I see a punching bag/game of tag/or scallywag
A zipper jammed/door slammed/closet crammed
Paint dabby/work shabby/knees scabby.

I think of you only now and then...only when...
I smell cookies, cakes/burgers, shakes/fries, steaks
See basketballs/postered walls/get collect calls
Walks with a slouch/sprawls on a couch/mother's
    grouch.

I think of you only now and then...only when...
I hear blasting guitars/speeding cars/noisy bars
See guys with a lopsided grin/bearded chin/wallet thin
Masses of hair/jeans threadbare/thumbing somewhere.

Yes, I think of you only now and then...only when...
I've something to share
I'm kneeling in prayer
Or breathing the air.

Joyce Clark
(used by author's permission)

The poem was an appropriate way for this hurting mother to express her pain and tell other people what she was going through.

LETTING OTHERS BLESS US

It was so difficult for me to talk about my own stress, strain, and pain during our daughter's prodigal years. But when I finally did share them with a friend, my friend said to me, "If I'd only known you were going through this, I could have prayed for you." Simply by staying quiet, I had denied myself the blessing of her friendship and her prayers.

Not only do we lose the blessing of the friendship and the support of other people, but we also neglect helping other people who are going through similar experiences. God can use us to help others when we are willing to risk the pain of telling the truth. As others are going through that first week of panic and pain, we can share our experiences and friendship.

"A friend loves at all times, and a brother is born for adversity" (Proverbs 17:17). When people are going through emotional pain, their burden is eased by friends and family who are willing to reach out and help.

"I know what it's like to live in the courtyard of hell," said one mother, whose son went on a crime spree that landed him in prison. The woman was overwhelmingly emotionally sustained by her Christian friends, whose prayers and comfort made it possible for her to survive that harrowing ordeal.

Getting involved with other hurting parents can bring unusual and unexpected side effects. As I began writing this book, I discovered deeply buried wounds that were still raw and bleeding. As other families shared their pain with me, my own wounds throbbed in response. As their tears flowed, so did mine, and something unusual happened. Slowly, my raw wounds began to heal. Shared pain became shared gain, and with the healing has come a firm resolve to reach out quickly to other parents and families who are going through the painful prodigal years.

BLESSING OTHERS

Getting involved can be as simple as pouring a cup of tea during a quiet moment. In the intimacy of that shared moment, you can invite the other parent to tell you about his or her prodigal child.

One of the greatest ways to reach out to other people is to simply let them talk about their problem. When the problem is bottled up inside of them, it becomes a continuing, painful burden. Everyone needs the opportunity to pour out the stress he or she has been going through. It isn't so much that we have such wonderful advice to give; it is simply giving people the opportunity to talk.

"Letting them talk is a very large part of it," Carol added. "I just shared what had happened with Debbie. I didn't offer any advice. I just let them know that they do come out at the other end of the tunnel. That's been my theme…it's going to be okay. I can't say when, but at some point, it's going to be okay."

Reaching out to other hurting families is an act of love. As the adage says, "Actions speak louder than words." Sometimes we need to act rather than speak. We can by our actions express God's love to other hurting parents. One church family decided to give a baby shower for an unwed teenage mother as an expression of God's love to her. Their action tremendously helped the parents to feel the support of their Christian friends. That action showed love and acceptance for the child. As the Bible admonishes us, we are to hate the sin and love the sinner.

Acts of love do not need to be large to be effective. A small note of encouragement or a card that simply says, "I'm praying for you," can be effective. Whatever we choose to do, it is important that we do something to reach out to others.

God doesn't want us to waste our suffering. When we are willing to be open to others, He can use our pain to bring help and support to those who need it the most.

"It's been a year and a half since Ryan died," said Bob (refer to Chapter 11). "We get letters from Compassionate Friends, an organization that deals with people who have lost children. Ryan had been away from home for almost thirteen years before he succumbed to acute alcoholism."

"When friends of ours lost a son in a car accident, they weren't suprised when we came to call," said Gayle. "Their first words to us were, 'We wondered when you would come.' It was neat to be able to sit and visit with them. They knew that we would understand."

GLORIFYING GOD

Our suffering is never wasted when others benefit from our lessons and experience. When we tell other people how God has helped us to survive the prodigal years, we are glorifing His name: "One generation will commend your works to another; they will tell of your mighty acts" (Psalm 145:4).

We praise Him well when we tell other people what He has done in our lives. As we tell other people what God has done for us, it offers them hope and wisdom and understanding. It encourages them to turn to God for their strength and guidance.

As we stand alongside other people and encourage them, we are fulfilling God's plan for our lives. By letting God use us in this way, we are allowing Him to take our suffering and our hardship and turn it into something good. "And we know that in all things God works for the good of those who love him, who have been called according to his purpose" (Romans 8:28).

Like a pebble dropped in a clear lake, the ripples travel outward. The more we share with other people about how God has helped us, the more we help other people. Our help then reaches farther and farther to still other people. The message we share is this: with God's help, we can survive the prodigal years.

■ ■ ■

1. Name a parent of a prodigal child. Meet with him or her this week to offer encouragement.

2. What act of God's love can you show toward a prodigal child?

3. Send a note or card of encouragement to a parent of a prodigal child.

Prayer To Pray

Lord, I've kept quiet for so long, hiding my pain. Help me to be willing to risk telling others about my exeriences so that Your name will be glorified. I know other people are hurting, too, and I want to help them. Guide me to show acts of love to them that will encourage them. Thank You for Your love that has helped me to survive these prodigal years. Amen.

Promise To Claim

"In all these things we are more
than conquerors through him who loved us."

(Romans 8:37)

APPENDIX

RUNAWAY AND SUICIDE HOTLINE   1-800-621-4000
RUNAWAY HOTLINE   1-800-231-6946
COCAINE HELPLINE   1-800-COCAINE
CONFIDENTIAL COCAINE REFERRAL LINE   1-800-662-HELP
   (refers callers to cocaine abuse centers and provides free materials
   on drug abuse)
"DIRECTORY OF RUNAWAY PROGRAMS"   1-202-755-7800
   (order a free copy)
   Division of Runaway Youth Programs
   Administration of Children, Youth and Families
   Department of Health and Human Services
   P.O. Box 1182
   Washington, DC 20013
JUVENILE JUSTICE CLEARINGHOUSE   1-800-638-8736
   (publications, information referrals)
WISCONSIN CLEARINGHOUSE   1-800-262-6243
   (free catalog of resources of materials   1-608-263-2797
   on alcohol abuse, drug education, and mental health)

P.O. Box 1468
Madison, WI 53701
(ask for health information clearinghouse)
TOUGHLOVE   1-800-333-1069
P.O. Box 1069   1-215-7090
Doylestown, PA 18901
   (help for parents with children who are demonstrating inappro-
   priate behavior)
JUST SAY NO FOUNDATION   1-800-369-2766
1777 North California Boulevard
Suite 210
Walnut Creek, CA 94596
   (programs for children ages 7 - 14;
   formation of "Just Say No" clubs)
SCHOOL CHALLENGE CAMPAIGN   1-800-624-0100
   (brochures and information to develop   1-800-541-8787
   drug-prevention programs
KEEPING DRUGS OUT OF THE SCHOOLS (order free information)
Dept. 502R
Consumer Information Center
Pueblo, CO 81009
DRUG EDUCATION INFORMATION   1-202-633-1469
Office of Public Affairs   (order free information)
Drug Enforcement Administration
Department of Justice
1405 I Street N.W., Room 1209
Washington, DC 20537
TRENDS IN DRUG USE   1-202-633-1316
Information Systems Unit   (information available)
Office of Diversion Control
Drug Enforcement Administration
Department of Justice
1405 I Street N.W.
Washington, DC 20537
COMMUNITY INTERVENTION, INC.   1-800-328-0417
529 S. Seventy Street, Suite 570   1-612-332-6537
Minneapolis, MN 55415   (free publications and catalog)
EDUCATIONAL MATERIALS ON ALCOHOL AND OTHER DRUGS
Hazelden Educational Materials   (free catalog)   1-800-328-9000
Box 176
Pleasant Valley Road
Center City, MN 55012

DRUG ABUSE INFORMATION
    For information   1-301-468-2600
    For drug abuse treatment and referral   1-800-662-HELP
PARENTS' RESOURCE INSTITUTE   1-800-241-9746
    FOR DRUG EDUCATION (PRIDE)   1-404-577-4500
National Parents' Resource Institute for Drug Education, Inc.
50 Hurt Plaza, Suite 210
Atlanta, GA 30303
MATERNAL AND CHILD HEALTH DATA BOOK   1-202-628-8787
    (book on the complex factors affecting infant health,
    teen pregnancies, etc.)
Children's Defense Fund
122 C Street N.W.
Washington, DC 20001
AIDS HOTLINE   1-800-638-6252
101 West Read Street, Suite 825
Baltimore, MD 21201
    (refers to testing sites and counseling)
PHS AIDS HOTLINE   (Public Health Service)
1-800-342-AIDS
1-800-243-7889   (Voice/TDD)
1-800-344-7432   (Spanish)
NATIONAL AIDS NETWORK   1-202-293-2437
    (support organization)
2033 M Street N.W., Suite 800
Washington, DC 20036
ORTON DYSLEXIA SOCIETY
1-800-222-3123
1-301-296-0232
AMERICAN ANOREXIA/BULIMIA ASSOCIATION   1-201-836-1800
BASH, Selfhelp for Anorexics and Bulimics
1-800-762-3334 / 1-800-227-4785
CHILDHOOD OBESITY   1-301-496-5133
NATIONAL ASSOCIATION OF   1-312-831-3438
    ANOREXIA NERVOSA AND ASSOCIATED DISORDERS
OVEREATERS ANONYMOUS   1-213-542-8363